Block Island: Map And Guide, Historic Sketch

Samuel Truesdale Livermore

In the interest of creating a more extensive selection of rare historical book reprints, we have chosen to reproduce this title even though it may possibly have occasional imperfections such as missing and blurred pages, missing text, poor pictures, markings, dark backgrounds and other reproduction issues beyond our control. Because this work is culturally important, we have made it available as a part of our commitment to protecting, preserving and promoting the world's literature. Thank you for your understanding.

BLOCK ISLAND.

I. A MAP AND GUIDE.
II. A HISTORY (Abridged).

BY

REV. S. T. LIVERMORE, A.M.

HARTFORD, CONN.:
PRESS OF THE CASE, LOCKWOOD & BRAINARD COMPANY.
1882.

COPYRIGHTED
BY S. T. LIVERMORE,
1882.

THE SPRING HOUSE, BLOCK ISLAND, R. I.
Hon. B. B. Mitchell, Proprietor.

THE SPRING HOUSE.

More than thirty years ago the SPRING HOUSE, the pioneer of Block Island Hotels, first opened its doors to the public under the management of Captain Alfred Card. For nearly twenty years, while other Hotels opened only to close again, the SPRING HOUSE continued, as season followed season, the only Hotel to open its doors to the public, thereby not only laying the foundation for the reputation Block Island now enjoys as a Summer resort, but also establishing itself as the most popular Family Hotel upon the Atlantic coast.

Some thirteen years since, the SPRING HOUSE passed into the hands of its present management, and in the meantime has been greatly improved and enlarged, until to-day the names of some of the first people of our State and country, found recorded year after year upon the register of the SPRING HOUSE, can attest to its reputation and popularity.

The SPRING HOUSE is situated upon the eastern shore of Block Island, one-eighth of a mile from the landing, thereby being removed from the immediate noise and confusion incidental to the arrival and departure of steamers, the landing and embarking of passengers and the loading and unloading of freight, a fact parents and invalids will readily notice and appreciate.

Arriving at the landing, we may reach the SPRING HOUSE by taking the coach, which connects with all boats, and following Main Street a short distance turn into Spring Street, at the head of which avenue the Hotel stands; or, should you prefer, you may turn to the eastward, stroll along the bluffs which border the Atlantic Ocean, and after a walk of five minutes, the surf breaking over the beach just below your feet, you find yourself upon the broad piazza which surrounds the SPRING HOUSE.

To the eastward the ground slopes to the shores of the broad Atlantic, upon the bosom of which may be seen the sail of the coaster and the black smoke of the passing steamer, while in the immediate foreground are seen the famous Springs from which the Hotel takes its name, which supply the Hotel with pure and healthful water, and which are the sole property of the proprietor of the SPRING HOUSE, this being the only Hotel upon the Island supplied with spring water.

To the south, one mile distant, may be seen the well-known "Southeast Light," the most powerful light of the first class, upon the Atlantic coast. An excellent opportunity for bass-fishing is afforded from this side of Block Island.

To the west we look out over the Island and Long Island Sound.

To the north, some fifty feet below us, the well-known Ocean View Hotel appears. Beyond may be seen the harbor, breakwater, and Clay Head.

For rest, quiet, and pure ocean breeze, no place can be found to surpass the SPRING HOUSE, Block Island, while our genial host, B. B. MITCHELL, Esq., a gentleman who has for several years past represented his town in the General Assembly of Rhode Island, and his excellent wife, render everything within doors most agreeable, comfortable, and attractive, and no one passes out from the cool, bright hall-way of the SPRING HOUSE during the warm season, but does so with the determination of returning again as soon as possible.

B. B. MITCHELL, Proprietor.

Ocean View Hotel.

This Popular Home on the Ocean stands on a beautiful green bluff, nearly one hundred feet above the surf, where it is fanned perpetually by the salt-laden breezes from the bracing waters of the Atlantic. Its broad piazzas (extending over 400 feet in length) command a magnificent view of ocean and rural scenery.

GAS AND ELECTRIC BELLS.—Every room in the hotel is lighted with gas, and communicates with the office by the most improved system of electric bells.

The hotel is furnished with bath-rooms, post-office, news-stand, daily mails, library, hair-dressing rooms, steam laundry, large play-room for children, etc.

OCEAN VIEW COTTAGE.

This elegant Double Cottage has been built especially for families who desire the quiet and privacy of their own homes.

It is situated on high grounds overlooking the ocean and harbor; contains twenty-four sleeping-rooms and two parlors, and has a broad piazza nearly 100 feet in length.

The Cottage is lighted with gas, is supplied with running water, and communicates with the OCEAN VIEW office by electric bells.

The very extensive additions to the OCEAN VIEW, its greatly improved dining-room, halls and parlors, just completed for the Summer of 1882, are part of the evidence of its proprietor's and its manager's determination to please its former and its new patrons the coming season.

TABLE.—All kinds of Sea-Food, the famous Block Island blue-fish, cod-fish, sword-fish, bass, lobsters, etc., are caught within sight of the hotel, and served in every possible style.

The fruits, meats, etc., come daily from the best markets; the lambs, chickens, milk, cream, vegetables, etc., are supplied from the numerous Island farms. *The table and service will be kept at the highest standard.*

PURE WATER.—A pure spring supplies the whole house with delicious drinking water.

DRAINAGE.—As the OCEAN VIEW stands nearly 100 feet above the ocean, the drainage is *absolutely perfect*.

AMUSEMENTS.

LAWN GAMES.—A beautiful lawn, surrounding the hotel, extends clear to the edge of the bluff; where the lovers of *tennis, croquet, base-ball, foot-ball, etc.*, may indulge, at noonday, beneath a summer sun, without the slightest discomfort from oppressive heat.

EVENING ENTERTAINMENTS, ETC.—Music will be furnished by the Hotel Orchestra, and no pains will be spared to make the evening entertainments, which have become so popular in the Parlors of the OCEAN VIEW, more enjoyable this season than ever before.

Probably there is no hotel in the country where young and old together more thoroughly enjoy themselves, in innocent sports and healthful amusements, than at the OCEAN VIEW; and it is the constant and determined aim of the management to contribute in every possible way to the real comfort and happiness of the guests, and to make this "Emerald dot on the Ocean" a delightful *Summer Home.*

NICHOLAS BALL, Proprietor.
O. S. MARDEN, Manager.

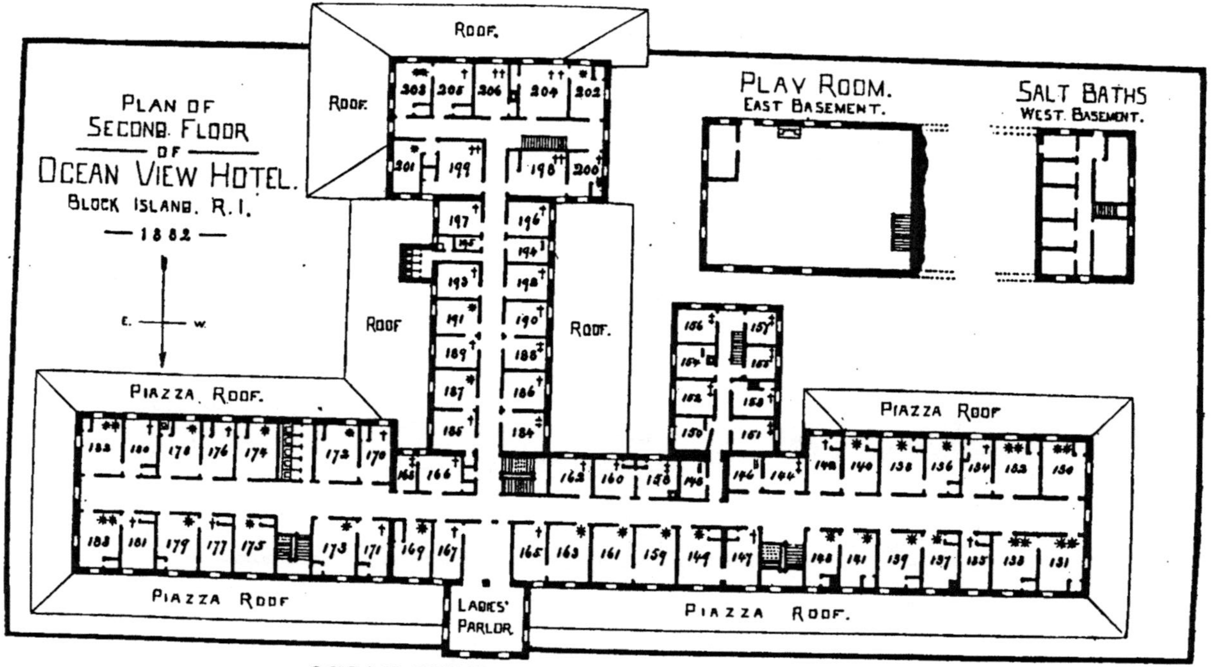

OCEAN VIEW HOTEL, BLOCK ISLAND, R. I.

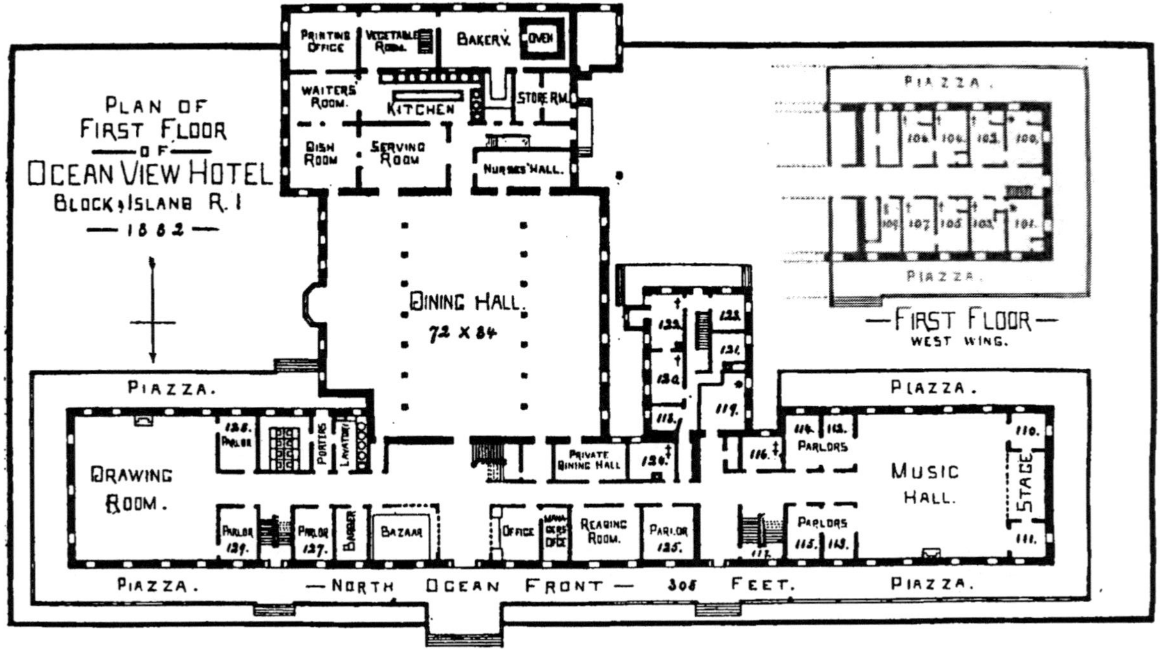

OCEAN VIEW HOTEL, BLOCK ISLAND, R. I.

CONNECTICUT HOUSE, BLOCK ISLAND, R. I. M. M. Day, Proprietor.

CONNECTICUT HOUSE,

BLOCK ISLAND.

This House has an elevated location, commanding fine views of land and water, ocean and mainland, from nearly every window. It is quiet and restful, on Main Street, surrounded with green and fragrant fields, convenient to Post-Office, Telegraph, and Bathing-Beach, which is reached by a private way, free from dust.

Carriages, on arrival of Steamers, to Convey Guests to the House, Free.

At the Wharf inquire for the CONNECTICUT HOUSE, and expect prompt attention.

TERMS MODERATE.

M. M. DAY, - - - Proprietor.

THE HIGHLAND HOUSE, BLOCK ISLAND, R. I.
D. M. MITCHELL, Proprietor.

HIGHLAND HOUSE,

BLOCK ISLAND.

This new and well-appointed House, within a quarter of a mile of the Landing, has a very high and beautiful location, commanding picturesque views of the Island, and most extensive ocean and mainland scenery. Its grounds are ample for the various kinds of out-door games in the refreshing breezes of summer.

BOARD AND ROOMS AT REASONABLE PRICES.

Located on High Street.

D. M. MITCHELL, - Proprietor.

PROMPT ATTENTION TO GUESTS ON ARRIVAL AT THE WHARF.

STEAMER GEO. W. DANIELSON, BLOCK ISLAND, R. I.

BLOCK ISLAND STEAMBOAT CO.

New Line between Providence and Block Island,

VIA NEWPORT AND CONTINENTAL LINE,

Carrying United States Mail.

THE NEW AND STAUNCH STEAMER,

1882 GEO. W. DANIELSON, 1882

Capt. CONLEY,

Is running Daily, Sundays excepted, between Block Island and Newport, connecting with Steamers of the Continental Line to Providence.

Leave Block Island at 8 A.M., arriving at Newport in time to connect with Steamer for Providence at 11.20 A.M.

Passengers for Block Island can take the Steamer at Providence, arriving at Newport at 12 M., connecting with Steamer from Block Island at 12.30 P.M.

All express matter for Block Island will be shipped by Earl & Prew's Express.

All Deposits of Freight to be marked "Block Island, via Continental Line."

[SEE PAGE 12.]

CONNECTIONS.

All the railroads that enter Boston connect with the Old Colony to Newport, and the various roads to Providence, and thence with steamers to Block Island.

Railroads and Sound Steamers from New York to Providence and Newport also connect with steamers to Block Island.

Steamer direct from Norwich and New London to Block Island, where time tables are kept at the hotels.

STEAMER

GEO. W. DANIELSON,

Capt. CONLEY,

Leaves Block Island daily at 8 A.M. for Newport, and connects directly with steamer to Providence.

Leaves Newport for Block Island on arrival of steamer from Providence, at 12.30 P.M.

INDEX.

	Page.		Page
Aborigines,	47	Grove Point,	26
Arrests,	60	Golden Grove—brig,	100
Bay, Block Island,	42	Harbor,	20
Bathing Beach,	31	Harbor Hill,	22
Breach, The,	42	Harbors,	75
Briton's Rock,	41	Harbor Pond,	36
Beacon Hill,	24	Hostilities,	52
Block Island Sound,	41	" Indian,	53
		" French,	55
		" English,	53
Cemetery, The,	30	Hotels,	9
Centre, The,	22		
Cow Cove,	41	Inhabitants,	50
Clay Head,	26	Indian-Head-Neck,	27
Churches,	120		
Charlestown Wreck—poetry,	114	Life Saving Stations,	12
Chagum Pond,	34	Light Houses,	9
Call, First Minister's,	121	Library,	119
		Legends,	88
Danielson, G. W.—steamer,	12	Location,	46
Dorry's Cove,	43		
Discovery,	46	Meeting Houses,	123
Dancing Mortar,	89	Mohegan Bluffs,	23
		Mails,	13
Fort Island,	28	Mortar,	89
Fog Signal,	11	Mill Pond,	37
Fresh Pond,	34	Middle Pond,	35
Fisheries,	65	Moluncus—brig,	82
French, The,	55	Messer, Laura E.,	85
		Mays, The,	84
Grace's Cove,	43		
Great Pond,	32	Names of the Island,	48

INDEX.

	Page.		Page.
Old Harbor,	42	Sound, Block Island,	41
		Signal Station,	14
Phrases, Sailor,	74	Schools,	119
President Grant's Visit,	120	Sands Pond,	34
Phantom Ship,	106	Surface,	49
Palatine Legend,	92	Springs,	38
Poetry,	106	Steamer, First,	12
Pleasure Fishing,	38		
Products,	49	Tempest, Sudden,	71
Possession,	57	Trimm's Pond,	37
Petition to R. I. Assembly,	57		
Palmer, Rev. A. G., D.D.,	106	Whittier,	101
		Willey, Dr.,	96
Revolutionary,	58	Wrecks,	78
Refugees,	61	Wrecking,	84
		War of 1812,	63
Sandy Hill,	25	Whales,	73
Sandy Point,	26	Warrior, wrecked,	80

PREFACE.

THE object of this book is to answer the rapidly increasing inquiries concerning Block Island. To do this special effort has been made to have the map and the guide accurate and instructive to strangers. Its historical and legendary part, it is believed, will furnish instruction and amusement enough to compensate the reader for the price paid for the Map, Guide, and History.

If the author is correct in these estimates, there is good reason for his expectation of a double reward for his labor, *first* in the hope of benefiting and pleasing the public, and *secondly* in obtaining from them a liberal patronage.

Believing that all things are given us "richly to enjoy," and that those are happiest who do the most to make others happy, the writer anticipates much from the conviction that this little book will guide many to one of the most attractive sources of health, rest, and pleasure that can be found upon the coast of the Atlantic. After a residence upon Block Island of four winters and three summers, he has here given some of the results of his study of old authentic records, and of careful observation, much of which is taken from his History of Block Island published in 1877, and now nearly out of print.

As so much of that history is here incorporated the following notice, as a sample of many others, is taken from the Woonsocket *Patriot* of March, 1881.

"*A History of Block Island* from its discovery in 1824 to the present time; by Rev. S. T. Livermore, A.M.

"The growing popularity of Block Island as a place of summer resort makes a good history of that Island desirable at this time. A perusal of the above-named book will convince the reader that the author has been thorough and painstaking in the investigation of old records and collecting of other material for the work, and a halo of interest is thrown around the Island, such as no visit to its shores or legend of the 'Fire Ship' can awaken in the mind of the visitor unaided by this faithful and highly interesting account of this attractive "sea-girt isle." Do you contemplate a visit to Block Island? Take this book with you."

Criticisms and suggestions for the improvement of future editions will be thankfully received.

S. T. LIVERMORE.

Bridgewater, Mass.,
April, 1882.

BLOCK ISLAND.

HOTELS.

The first hotel for boarders from abroad was opened in 1842 by *Mr. Alfred Card*, one hundred and eighty years from the first settlement by sixteen families. It stood where the Adrian House is now located. There Mr. Card "set the first excursion table for boarders of pleasure" ever furnished on the Island. His first party consisted of seven men from Newport, one of whom was Mr. Van Buren. They remained two days, and " they were the first party that ever employed, at Block Island, a boat and boatmen to carry them a fishing." Mr. Card says, — "John L. Mitchell and Samuel W. Rose carried them out."

Fifteen years afterwards, in 1857, there were three hotels for the accommodation of visitors and boarders. These would lodge about one hundred. Since then they have increased in number and capacity until Block Island, as a summer resort, ranks among the first in popularity on the coast of the Atlantic.

LIGHT HOUSES.

The first Light House on Block Island was located on Sandy Point, the northerly extremity, and was erected by the Government in the year 1829. Its keeper was William Weeden, previously of Jamestown, R. I. It was serviceable less than ten years.

The second light-house was built upon the same point, in 1837. It was a substantial building, located in a less exposed position than was the first, farther inland. It had two towers, and its lights were exposed from them by parabolic reflectors. Mr. W. A. Weeden was its keeper until 1839, when he resigned and was succeeded by Mr. Simeon Babcock, who was succeeded in 1841 by Mr. Edward Mott by appointment of President Harrison. This house served about twenty years.

The third light-house was erected on the point in 1857, was kept by Mr. E. Mott until 1865 when Simeon Babcock was replaced by President Polk. This house stood the storms about ten years only. These three houses, all built within thirty years, were rendered useless by the shifting sands on which they were located.

The fourth light-house, and the one now in use on Sandy Point, was built in 1867. It is stone, well built, and protected so as to give promise of long and valuable service. Mr. Hiram D. Ball, brother of the proprietor of the Ocean View Hotel on the Island has kept the lights on the Point since 1861, then appointed by President Lincoln.

This last light-house is a favorite resort of visitors who reach it by the Neck Road from the Harbor, and by Main Street and Cemetery Street.

The new light-house is situated on the south-east corner of the Island which is triangular in form, as described by its first discoverer in 1524. At that angle the land is elevated, and the light conspicuous far at sea. It stands on a bluff one hundred and twenty-feet above mean low-water. Its lantern is fifty-two feet above the ground, and two hundred and four feet above the sea. It is of brick, and was erected in the summer of 1874 by Mr. L. H. Tynan, of Staten Island, at a cost of $75,000. The glass of the lantern cost the Government $10,000, and consists mainly of prismatic lenses scientifically arranged to produce the best effect. Six persons at the same time can stand within this lantern. It has been seen thirty-five miles, and was first lighted February

TO THE NEW LIGHT HOUSE.

1, 1875. It consumes one thousand gallons of oil annually, burning four circular wicks, one within another, the largest about three and a half inches in diameter, the least seven-eighths inches in diameter.

Aside from the attractions of the new light-house itself, whose first keeper was Mr. H. W. Clark, whose courtesy to thousands of visitors is remembered with pleasure, the landscape scenery there, and while going and coming, and the extensive view out upon the ocean well repay the visitors. The route there from the harbor is southerly, up High Street and by Dodge Street nearly to Sands Pond, thence easterly by cart track and gates across several farms. Distance from the harbor about three miles, and a good road most of the way. The light-house stands near the place where the Mohegan captives were starved by the Maniseans, long before the Island was settled by the English. There Mr. Clark has charge of the Light, the Fog Signal, and the Storm Signals.

THE FOG SIGNAL.

This, as well as the light-houses and life-saving stations, is a Government institution, and is connected with the new light-house, separated from it about one hundred feet. It is under the superintendence of the keeper of the light-house, and is blown to warn mariners to avoid the Island in fogs and storms when the light is of little avail. It is sounded by the steam of a four-horse power engine, two of such being kept in readiness for service. The sound is made in immense trumpets, directed towards the sea, seventeen feet long, of cast metal. The trumpet does not *make*, but directs the sound which originates from the *siren*, or buzz in the small end of the trumpet, the larger end of which is about five feet in diameter. The siren, made of brass, strong, is struck by the current of steam and made to revolve with so great velocity as to make the sound that goes out through the fogs and storms over the sea to warn the mariner of his approach to danger. Whoever stands near that fog-horn when sounding will not be surprised that ships are frightened away. It once made a deaf mute jump and run for dear life.

LIFE-SAVING STATIONS.

Two of these are upon the Island, one at the harbor, and the other at Cooneymus, on the west side. The former was established in 1872, at an expense of about $2,000, including "gear," and the latter at greater expense was erected in 1874. Each accommodates seven expert sailors, one of them being captain, and they patrol the shores each night through the winter, watching for vessels in distress. These stations are furnished with cooking-stoves, tables, dormitories, beds, and the best modern appliances for saving those in peril, on the sea, near the shore. Annual expense about $3,000.

FIRST STEAMER.

The first permanent Block Island steamer, the *George W. Danielson*, built by the Block Island Steamboat Company, was launched at Mystic, Conn., in May, 1880. Her first trip on her regular line from Block Island to Newport and Providence was made June 15, 1880, and it was one of the great events of the Island when she took the place of the Island schooners and of the frail masted open boats in which passengers were exposed to all sorts of weather, to head winds and to calms. She was built with special reference to the heavy seas of winter and the comfort of pleasure-seekers in summer. She has proved herself very staunch and convenient. Her masts not only add to her speed, but are a means of safety in case of failure in her machinery. She is manned by the best of sailors. Her commander, Captain George W. Conley, a christian gentleman of great experience at sea, formerly master of a first-class coaster, is cautious, brave, and strictly temperate. No better man could be found for his position. This he has shown in the selection of his mate, Mr. B. F. Gardner, his engineer, Mr. George W. Braymon, his purser, Mr. M. V. Ball, and his steward, Mr. Frank Masard.

In 1881, mostly in the summer, the *G. W. Danielson* carried over 7,000 passengers. Her times of leaving and arrival may be seen in the time table of the guide. She carries the mail between Providence, Newport, and Block Island.

THE MAILS OF BLOCK ISLAND.

One hundred and seventy years after Block Island was colonized by settlers from Massachusetts its first regular mail was established. Previous to that letters reached its inhabitants through the post-office at Newport, and the letters from the Island were mailed at various places visited by the Islanders while marketing their fish and produce. Their first post-master, *William L. Wright*, was appointed December 13, 1832, and his office was his bed-room. From that date up to 1876 the arrival of the mail was the great event of the Island. Then news by letters and papers was fresh "from America." As the mail was opened a circle of faces gathered around, and by a custom kept up more than forty years the whole Island was duly informed of the arrival of each letter, whether of love or business. For the postmaster proclaimed to the anxious listeners the name of each person addressed, and his hearers from all parts of the Island carried home and reported the news of the last arrivals. It was customary for one neighbor to answer for several others who were absent from the calls of the postmaster at the distribution.

The first contractor for carrying the Block Island mail was Captain Samuel W. Rose, on a salary of $416 a year, leaving the Island on Wednesday morning at eight o'clock, and returning from Newport at the same hour on Thursday. Captain Rose was succeeded by his son *Captain John E. Rose*, who, rather than be underbid by his competitor, contracted to carry the mail to Newport for *one cent a year*, and after four years of faithful service to the Government he had received only *one cent* of the four due, and that *one* was paid by a Providence gentleman who wanted the honor of paying from his own pocket the whole expense of carrying the Block Island mail one year. Now, in summer, the mails are daily, and part of the time several each day, and the Islanders, by their own steamer and telegraph, are thoroughly identified with *other nations*.

THE SIGNAL STATION.

This, like the Wolf Head Light off Land's End, has converted a place of former disaster into a means of safety. That light is founded upon a sunken rock which rises in deep water like a tower to the surface in low tide, and for centuries was the terror of all navigators of the English Channel. Now it supports the most valuable beacon of the channel. So Block Island, on which hosts of wrecks have occurred, now atones for her past offences by displaying signals of warning to the vast processions of vessels almost constantly in sight of her shores.

The establishment of this station was an event of so much importance to the public and to the Island that a record of its incipient steps is here deemed appropriate, the enterprise, like that of securing the Breakwater and the Life Saving Stations, and the New Light-House, originating on the Island.

The following letter, with accompanying petition, was forwarded to various commercial houses and cities along the Atlantic coast, and to the Chamber of Commerce, New York, besides to various boards of trade : —

THE SIGNAL STATION.

BLOCK ISLAND, R. I., OCT. 20, 1875.

I wish to call your attention to the benefits to be derived from a Signal Station located upon this Island.

The Station would probably be where the New Light now is, upon the southern bluffs of the Island. There are frequently 200 sail of vessels passing near these bluffs at one time, and there is no place on our whole Atlantic coast more exposed, or where the signal of foul or fair weather would be greeted by so many vessels.

The cable, necessarily connected with it, might be used, in addition to its regular despatches, for the purpose of telegraphing news of vessels bound in or out, wrecks or disabled vessels, and such other news as would be of national interest. It also would be of local value, so much so as to probably be self-sustaining.

Again : Since the Government Breakwater has been constructed, the fishing interests have grown largely, so that during the fishing seasons of Spring and Autumn, a hundred or more fishing crafts are about the Island. To them the Signal would be of great value.

In view of the above facts, will you please take some interest in having the inclosed petition signed by the commercial men in your city and then forward it directly to the Representative in Congress for your district?

Respectfully yours,

NICHOLAS BALL.

To the Honorable the Senate and House of Representatives in Congress assembled.

We, the undersigned, who have a special interest in the shipping business transacted along the whole Atlantic Coast, do hereby petition the Honorable Senate and House of Representatives of the United States for the establishment of a Signal Station on Block Island, to be connected with the main shore by a telegraphic cable.

The cost of such a station and cable would be but little compared with their great importance to the commerce of the country ; and we are assured that their necessity has already been recognized by various officials of the Government, among whom may be mentioned the distinguished President of the Light House Board, Professor Joseph Henry.

CHAMBER OF COMMERCE OF THE STATE OF NEW YORK,
NEW YORK, Nov. 5, 1875.

NICHOLAS BALL, ESQ., —

Dear Sir, — Your note of the 20th ult., with the enclosed Memorial to Congress in regard to the establishment of a Signal Station on Block Island, was submitted to the Chamber of Commerce at its meeting yesterday, and referred for report to its Committee on Commerce and Revenue Laws.

Your obedient servant,

GEORGE WILSON, *Secretary*.

CHAMBER OF COMMERCE OF THE STATE OF NEW YORK,
NEW YORK, DEC. 7, 1875.

Dear Sir, — The petition to Congress for the establishment of a Signal Station on Block Island was unanimously approved by the Chamber of Commerce, at its meeting on Thursday last, and ordered to be transmitted to that body.

In addition to the signature of the President of the Chamber to the petition, we have obtained the names of the Presidents of all the Marine Insurance Companies of this city, and of the leading shipping merchants engaged in the eastern trade.

Your obedient servant,

GEORGE WILSON, *Secretary*.

NICHOLAS BALL, ESQ.

CHAMBER OF COMMERCE OF THE STATE OF NEW YORK,
NEW YORK, DEC. 10, 1875.

Dear Sir, — In response to your request of the 6th inst., I enclose herewith a copy of the proceedings of the Chamber at a meeting held on the 2d inst., relative to the establishment of a Signal Station on Block Island.

Your obedient servant,

GEORGE WILSON, *Secretary*.

NICHOLAS BALL, ESQ.

Extract from proceedings of the Chamber of Commerce, New York, at its monthly meeting, held December 2, 1875 :—

The regular monthly meeting of the Chamber of Commerce was held Thursday, Dec. 2, 1875, at one o'clock, P.M., at the rooms of the Chamber, No. 63 William St. Present: Samuel D. Babcock, Esq., and a quorum of members.

* * * * * * *

Mr. James W. Elwell, Chairman of the Committee on Foreign Commerce and the Revenue Laws, to whom was referred at the last meeting of the Chamber the communication of Mr. Nicholas Ball, with the accompanying petition to Congress for the establishment of a Signal Station on Block Island, submitted a report on the subject, which was unanimously adopted and ordered to be placed on file, and the petition forwarded to Congress as recommended by the Committee.

[Attest.]   GEORGE WILSON, *Secretary.*

(*A copy of the Report and Memorial are appended herewith.*)

To the Chamber of Commerce:

Your Committee on Foreign Commerce and the Revenue Laws, to whom was referred for consideration at the last meeting of the Chamber the communication of Mr. Nicholas Ball, with the accompanying petition to Congress for the establishment of a Signal Station on Block Island, beg leave to report, —

That the subject has received their careful attention, and the Committee are of the opinion that the establishment of such Signal Station is a necessity, and would be of great benefit to the commerce of the country. The Committee, in response to the request of Mr. Ball, have obtained the signatures of the President of the Chamber, the Presidents of all the Marine Insurance Companies, and of the principal shipping houses of the city, to the petition which they now submit for approval and presentation to Congress.

     JAMES W. ELWELL, *Chairman.*

NEW YORK, DEC 1, 1875.

[A true copy.]   GEORGE WILSON, *Secretary.*

THE CHAMBER OF COMMERCE OF THE STATE OF NEW YORK,

By SAMUEL D. BABCOCK, *President.*
JOHN D. JONES,
Pres. Atlantic Mutual Ins. Co.
F. S. LATHROP,
Pres. Union Mutual Ins. Co.
F. B. BLEECKER, JR.,
V. P. New York Mutual Ins. Co.
ALFRED OGDEN,
V. P. Orient Mutual Ins. Co.
ALEX. MACKAY,
V. P. Great Western Ins. Co.
J. P. PAULISON,
Pres. Sun Mutual Ins. Co.
JNO. K. MYERS,
Pres. Pacific Mutual Ins. Co.
DANIEL DRAKE SMITH,
Pres. Commercial Mutual Ins. Co.
ELWOOD WALTER,
Pres. Mercantile Mutual Ins. Co.
JAS. W. ELWELL & CO.,
Shipping Agents and Owners.
MURRAY, FERRIS & CO.,
Agts. N. Y. & Sav., Nas. & Prov. Lines.
SNOW & BURGESS,
Agents & Owners.
OELRICKS & CO.,
Agents Bremen Line.
BORDEN & LOVELL,
New York.
OLD COLONY STEAMBOAT CO.,
per Borden & Lovell, New York.
FALL RIVER PROPELLER LINE,
Geo. Ketcham, Agent.
R. LOWDEN,
Agent Black Star Line of Steamships.

[A true copy.]   GEORGE WILSON, *Secretary.*

OFFICE OF THE BOSTON & PHILADELPHIA STEAMSHIPS,
BOSTON, DEC. 29, 1875.

MR. NICHOLAS BALL, —

Dear Sir, — Yours of the 27th received. The petition which you sent me has been signed by the agents of our Southern coastwise steam lines, and nearly all our Marine Insurance companies.

Yours truly,
E. B. SAMPSON, *Agent.*

WASHINGTON, D. C., Nov. 24, 1875.

MR. NICHOLAS BALL, —

Sir, — Your papers relating to the establishment of a Signal Service Station on Block Island having been referred to me, I will be glad to have you furnish me with a map or drawing showing in detail the position of the Island to the main land, and the various distances, so that I can calculate the amount of cable required to connect them.

Very respectfully,

H. H. C. DUNWOODY,
1st *Lieut. Fourth U. S. Artillery.*

Office of Chief Signal Officer A. S. O.,
Washington.

OFFICE OF THE CHIEF SIGNAL OFFICER,
WASHINGTON, D. C., Nov. 29, 1875.

MR. NICHOLAS BALL, —

Sir, — Your communication relative to the establishment of a Cautionary Signal Station at Block Island has been carefully considered by the Chief Signal Officer, who directs me to say that he regards the location as one which would doubtless prove of particular value as a Signal Station to both the shipping interests and the Signal Service.

The Charts showing the coast line in the vicinity of Block Island have been examined with a view of supplying you with an approximate estimate of the expense of securing telegraphic communication with the Island. The nearest direct line to the main land passes from the north extremity of the Island to a point about midway between Judith Point and Noys Point, a distance a little less than ten miles. From cable landing to the railroad, where it is presumed telegraphic connection may be made, is about five miles more, and with the five miles of wire on the Island, will require for the entire line, ten miles of cable at $1000 per mile, and say, twelve miles of wire at from $100 to $150 per mile.

Very respectfully,

H. H. C. DUNWOODY,
Lieut. A. S. O. and Asst.

The desired appropriation of $15,000 was made by Congress Dec. 19, 1879, and the cable was laid April 25, 1880, superintended by Lieut. James A. Swift, of the Signal Service, at the conclusion of which the Hon. Nicholas Ball delivered a brief and appropriate address to his fellow townsmen. Sergt. Wm. Davis, of the Signal Corps U. S. A., arrived upon the Island July 7th under orders from the Department to establish a full Meteorological Station, and on the 18th of July opened direct communication with Point Judith and Narragansett Pier, R. I. His first message was sent to Providence by Mr. C. E. Perry of the Island, and the first one received was from Capt. John E. Rose, also an Islander then at Narragansett Pier. The office was opened in the store of Mr. J. T. Dodge, at the Harbor. On the first of Sept., 1880, Sergt. Davis began taking and sending weather observations to the Department at Washington, D. C. On the 11th of March, 1881, the Block Island cable parted — cause unknown.

This Station displays its Signals on Harbor Hill, and at the New Light House, with which it has connection by telephone, and also with the Life Saving Station at the Harbor.

This telegraphic communication is of great value to summer guests, especially to business men, who can now regulate their visits by their knowledge of daily affairs at home. Yachting parties and all classes now can report arrivals and departures and other matters without delay.

THE HARBOR.

This is to Block Island what Liverpool is to England. It is almost a village. Here for centuries the treasures of the deep have been landed for the support of successive generations of the inhabitants. Here the old fishermen look with tearful eyes upon a few relics of the past and sigh over the encroachments of modern inventions. Here from childhood they have gone up and down the banks in the steps of their forefathers, have counted and dressed their fish as they did, and thence have wended their weary way homeward. Here they have enjoyed an excitement that could well dispense with the theater, the clubroom, the rat-pits of cities, the race-course and the regatta. Here, in spring, fall, and winter their fishing fleet have been launched and moored. Here many a race homeward has been sailed — not for a cup of gold, but for dear *life*, with a crowd of kindred upon the shore to rejoice over the safe landing of those pursued by the violent tempest.

Now, in summer, all is changed, as by the turn of the kaleidoscope. The fifteen-hundred-feet Government Breakwater, the wharf, the many steamers arriving and departing, with bells ringing and whistles blowing, the crowds of visitors coming and going, the rustling of silks and waving of white handkerchiefs from the high decks, the carriages now passing and repassing where the old fish houses once stood, the zealous information from the employees of a dozen hotels, the yachting parties hoisting sail, or coming into the basin, fishing parties arranging for "the banks," and the Island "High-hook" men exhibiting their twelve hundred blue fish just caught in their seine, while others with a less number taken with a troll are furnishing materials for the hotel tables, while the Bathing Beach is *alive* — all of this is a glimpse of the Harbor, near which are most of the hotels for summer visitors.

At the Harbor are stores, mechanic shops, the post-office, the signal station and telegraph, halls, and saloons, life saving station, etc. Here nearly all the shipping of the Island is transacted, and in one of its society halls religious services are conducted during the season of visitors. Here a chapel for accommodation of summer visitors is about to be built — the lot and funds in part having been subscribed.

THE CENTER.

This is located about a mile west of the Harbor. Here the people from all parts of the Island come for various purposes. The stores here do a large business. One of them, as well as one at the harbor, is an ornament to the Island, and attractive to visitors. At the Center are the town hall, the high school, the library, and the First Baptist Church. Here, too, is the old wind mill that has done good service since 1815 with its four arms, each thirty feet long, and here the people of the West Side market their fish, produce, eggs, poultry, sea-moss, etc.

The Centre may be visited directly from the harbor by Main Street, or by a drive down the Neck Road to Cemetery Street, and thence by the Great Pond and the Cemetery; or by High Street to Dodge Street, thence by Dodge Street to Coe's Gate, thence by cart track to the Fresh Pond, and thence by Centre Street to the Center. This last route affords very fine landscape, and distant water views.

HARBOR HILL.

But a part of this once-noted hill now remains. It is in the rear of the gothic cottage built by Mr. Darius Dodge a little west of the Harbor, on the right-hand corner as one turns from Main Street to go down the Neck Road. Much of that hill has been carried away by frosts, rains, and heavy seas. On it was a heavy battery in 1740 and previously to protect the Island against French and Spanish invasions. That battery commanded the Bay. Edward Sands was then "Captain of the Island," and had command of the quota of soldiers there. It was in reference to this battery on Harbor Hill that the R. I. Legislature enacted "That the six great guns at New Shoreham be mounted on carriages, in the most convenient manner, as shall be judged by the inhabitants; and that they, at their own charge, procure two barrels of gunpowder, one hund-

MOHEGAN BLUFFS, AND NEW LIGHT-HOUSE,
BLOCK ISLAND, R. I.

red and twenty great shot and forty pounds weight of musket balls." These great guns, and the military stores were removed to the main land at the beginning of the revolution. One of the cannon balls lingered upon the Island, was made a part of a wooden anchor for a light vessel in the Great Pond, after having been lost many years, was fished up there many years ago, and is now in the possession of the writer. That part of the Hill where the battery and earth works were probably located, was where the tide now ebbs and flows, and has disappeared like thousands of other strongholds that have been carried by the waves and tides of time into oblivion. From what remains of Harbor Hill one of the finest views may be had of the Bay and Harbor. There the Storm Signals of the Island are now displayed.

MOHEGAN BLUFFS.

These have been improperly called the *cliffs*. But Block Island never had any cliffs. Not even a ledge there has yet been discovered, without which there is no foundation for cliffs. These high bluffs are like those of Clay Head, with less impregnation of iron. When viewed from a short distance at sea they make a weird and pleasing impression, but are not comparable with those along the upper Mississippi, and in the vicinity of Omaha. Yet, to those not familiar with the more imposing heights the Mohegan Bluffs may well be considered grand, and pleasing, well repaying for a yacht excursion to the south-east of the Island, or for a walk to them at low tide along the east shore ; or for a ride to them by the road to the New Light House, viz. : by High Street, Dodge Street, and Cart Track from Sands' Gate.

These Bluffs took their name from the Mohegan Indian warriors who invaded the Island many centuries ago, were driven to these bluffs, cornered up there, and starved by the Manisseans, or Island Indians. This name applies to them all along the south shore from the New Light House to the vicinity of Black Rock. In the waters at their feet have been found very fine places for catching large bass with pole and reel. Expert fishermen have caught them there that weighed over sixty pounds. Favorable boulders can be reached at low tide.

BEACON HILL.

This is the highest land upon the Island, and is a miniature sugar loaf mountain. By a circuitous drive its summit can be reached with carriages. Many visitors, ladies and gentlemen, prefer to go there on foot. A strong, cool breeze will at all times give them an agreeable greeting. Its name originated from the light there used from time immemorial to warn the inhabitants of approaching enemies, especially during the old French and the Revolutionary wars. It was the rendezvous for Indians when they had their pow-wows and war-dances. There they assembled from time to time, drank rum, and bade defiance to their enemies at Montauk, and at Watch Hill where the fierce chief Sassacus and his bloody warriors looked with covetous eyes towards Manisses. It was there, evidently, that Thomas Terry by his strategy and fluent use of their language virtually disarmed them of their scalping knives as they were drinking rum and thinking of the sixteen families of white-faced intruders who were monopolizing their lands and fisheries. Mr. Terry knew they got their cask of rum of the trader Arnold then on the Island, and ingeniously, in their own tongue, wrought up their indignation towards the trader. When he had sufficiently fired their prejudice, as they made their wrathful, half-drunken protestations, seeing their cask of rum was on the verge of the "long descent to the bottom" of the hill, and that the bung was out of the cask, managing to have a strong Indian, then partially intoxicated, stand the upper side of the cask while Mr. Terry said to him, — "If you dislike Mr. Arnold, as you pretend, prove it by saying — *Tuckisha*, Mr. Arnold, and by giving his cask a hard kick."

With a savage yell the Indian exclaimed,—"*Tuckisha!* (I don't care for you) Mr. Arnold," and gave the cask so violent a kick that it went rolling down the hill and the rum escaping until it was all out, and that made the Indians *sober*, but not discerning enough to perceive the trick of wasting their rum.

From its summit the best view of the Island is obtained. One looks down upon it in all directions, and its undulating surface is very conspicuous, interspersed with its scores of ponds. The spectator sees the encircling waters of the ocean all around the Island, except at a small point near the new Light-house. There, too, one may see, in a clear atmosphere, with a good glass, Montauk, Stonington, Watch Hill, Point Judith, and Newport, and vessels in great numbers far at sea. The hill is about three hundred feet high.

To visit Beacon Hill from the Harbor, go to the Center, thence by Main Street to the foot of the hill on the right, where the bars are lowered for footmen, and removed for carriages.

SANDY HILL.

This is on the West Side, a little south of Grace's Cove, near the Sound shore. It is a pile of sand and gravel, in the form of a sugar-loaf or cone, rising about a hundred feet, with room on the top for a small pic-nic party, where there is a tuft of tall coarse grass in summer, and a constant sea breeze. It rests upon a thick bed of excellent peat, and is a study for the naturalist. It may be visited by following the shore north from Dorry's Cove, or by Cart-track from Main Street near the west foot of Beacon Hill.

SANDY POINT.

This is the northern extremity of the Island, and is pure sand. On it have been four successive light-houses. The first three were of brief service on account of their sandy foundation, which was disturbed by winds, waves, and tides. Too many have inferred that because it is sand all the Island is sandy and barren, which is a great mistake.

GROVE POINT.

This is a short distance easterly from Sandy Point, and many years ago projected much farther and more sharply into the sea than at present, and then made Cow Cove more distinct than it now is. Its name originated from the brig *Golden Grove*, which was wrecked upon it about a century ago, or about the time the Palatine visited the Island, not long before she was wrecked in the Bay of Bengal, according to authentic records. The Golden Grove was from Halifax, laden with pork and lard. Her captain, William Chitty, and his crew remained upon the Island, and when they and the Islanders wanted a barrel of pork they went to the wreck and helped themselves.

Her crew made up some doggerel poetry about their voyage, two lines of which are,—

"From Halifax, that frozen shore,
On Christmas day we made the shore
On Block Island, etc."

This "Christmas day" corresponds with the legend that the Palatine came ashore about Christmas.

The crew frequently celebrated their wreck, while repeating the following couplet:—

"Since on Block Island we saved our lives,
Here's health to our sweethearts and our wives."

CLAY HEAD.

This is the high, corrugated bluff seen on the northerly part of the Island while approaching it from Newport, and is that part nearest to Point Judith. It is the bold shore mentioned in Whittier's "Palatine," in the line,—

"The false lights over the Rocky Head!"

It is not rocky, but consists almost entirely of clay and sand, in which are a few boulders. Very fine qualities of blue, red, and white clay are found there, and some fantastic combinations of iron, clay, and sand, e. g., a mixture of clay tinged with iron forming itself around pure sand, from a gill to half a peck in quantity. The clay, with a small opening, hardens, the sands in time gradually escape out of the said opening, leaving behind them a few pebbles like birds' eggs, and these pebbles cannot pass out where the sand did, and these clay formations become simply stone shells, colored with iron, with pebbles rattling inside. The Islanders call the place where such have been abundant,—"*Pots and Kettles*" of Clay Head. This name sounds about as well as the more scientific *geode*.

One of the most pleasant walks of the Island, in the cool morning of summer, is from the Harbor along the Bathing Beach to the northerly part of Clay Head. To do this the visitor needs no guide—no directions more complex than the Boston boy gave to the English gentleman, as he replied to the latter,—"Keep this street and *follow your nose*." During this beautiful walk, you may see strange birds, shells, minerals, breakers, the sun rising out of the sea, and hear many strange sounds.

INDIAN-HEAD-NECK.

This narrow little bluff on the east shore of the south end of the Great Pond is a historic point of considerable interest. Here the Indians anciently buried their dead, and filled the graves with an ample supply of shell-fish from the adjacent Pond. The writer collected more than half a bushel of scallop shells from one grave opened by the frost in the bank facing the Pond, while spending a winter upon the Island. Some of the shells had never been opened, but were full of fine earth and sand, needing a little lime to make a petrifaction. Here, east of the road, lived the heroic Thomas Terry. On this Neck he disarmed, alone, thirty strange Indians, putting their guns in his house until they should leave the Island.

This Neck took its name from circumstances only partially understood. There, for some crime, anciently, two heads of Indians were placed upon stakes, sharpened at the top, and they remained in that condition. Tradition informs us that these two Indians were Mohegans or Pequots, and hence their heads were placed upon the stakes with their faces looking homeward, towards Stonington or Watch Hill. From their position the early settlers gave the bluff the name of *Indian-Head-Neck*. It is not far from the Bathing Beach, and is visited from the Harbor by going down the Neck Road to Cemetery Street on the left, and the bluff of the Neck is but a short distance from this intersection. From that old burying-place a fine view is had of the Great Pond and its surroundings, and of the ocean stretching far away with its many sails of commerce.

FORT ISLAND.

This little historic place is located a short distance south of the south end of the Great Pond, from which Trimm's Pond is separated by a narrow isthmus, on which Cemetery Street passes towards Indian-Head-Neck and Sandy Point. From this isthmus Fort Island is separated by a narrow channel but a few rods in width, while a considerable body of water is on its other sides. It is an elevated plat of about five acres, and is the property of Mr. Samuel Mott, whose house is the one nearest to the Island. It was occupied for a fort two hundred years ago, and how many centuries previous no record announces. It was doubtless a rude structure, consisting mainly of a breastwork around the little Island and elevated some distance from the water. To this the Manisseans could retreat when hard pressed by their invaders. The bloody battles there with the Mohegans, or with the Pequots long before the murder of Oldham and the capture of Block Island by Endicott, and its settlement by the English can easily be imagined. But in none of them, we are sure, was there ever displayed such heroism as the first settlers there exhibited, when neither a gun was fired, nor an arrow shot, nor a blow struck.

Three hundred native warriors, with guns, bows and arrows, scalping knives and tomahawks were still claiming homes on Block Island. It was aggravating for them to see their old corn plantations and fishing grounds monopolized by a few pale-faced foreigners, to have their lands and liberties taken from them without compensation, and to be made slaves. They knew their greater numbers and yet stood in awe of the greater sagacity of the white man. But their hostile feelings increased, and occasionally broke out in "insults, with threatening speeches, and offering smaller abuses," as reported by one intimate with eye-witnesses. With such feelings in three hundred savage breasts sixteen men and a boy had to contend, and they bravely challenged the whole Indian forces of the Island to meet them for a field fight. The Indian warriors accepted the challenge, and on the day appointed assembled on Fort Island. The defiant little army of seventeen marched bodly to the conflict. They were none the less brave though not a blow was struck. They expected to overawe their enemies by defiance, or were resolved to use their weapons to the best of their ability. Says Mr. Niles, one of the earliest inhabitants of the little colony, "Thither they came with utmost resolution, and war-like courage, and magnanimity."

During this procedure at Fort Island we can but faintly

imagine another scene which the historian cannot well describe. It was that assemblage of wives, mothers, and children at the Sand's Garrison, or stone house where there must have been the most painful anxieties over the issues of the day. If there were to be blood shed at Fort Island, what less than the scalping knife and the tomahawk could be expected by the helpless inmates of that garrison? But happily the prayers and tears and agonies there were all turned to rejoicing when the good news was heard of the peaceful capitulation. (See Hostilities.)

To visit Fort Island, now a cultivated field, go from the Harbor to the Center, thence by Cemetery Street to the south shore of the Great Pond, a short distance south of which the place of the ancient Fort is accessible.

THE CEMETERY.

The Block Island Cemetery, a quarter of a mile north of the Center, is on an elevation that overlooks much of the East Side, and of the Neck, and from it a fine water view is had of the Great Pond, Block Island Sound, Block Island Bay, and the Atlantic eastwards as far as the eye can reach. In this cemetery may be found some of the graves of the first and most prominent settlers. On a horizontal slab in the upper and central part of the grounds may be seen this Epitaph,—

HERE LYES INTERRED THE
BODY OF MR. JAMES SANDS SENIOR
AGED 73 YEARS WHO DEPARTED THIS
LIFE MARCH 13 A. D. 1695.

Near it is the grave of the venerable *Simon Ray*, designated by a gray stone slab on which is a long and honorable record of his virtues. He died in his one hundred and second year. There, too, may be seen the centenary grave of *Ackers Tosh*, and near the northwest corner of the cemetery are the seven graves of the passengers lost by the wreck of the *Warrior* on Sandy Point, and near them is the little grave of an unknown infant drowned and floated ashore from the wreck of the steamer *Metis* off Watch Hill.

The cemetery is visited by many, and is reached from the Harbor by going to the Center, and thence by Cemetery Street past the Wind Mill and Central House.

THE BATHING BEACH.

This is one of the principal attractions of the Island. The sand is fine, clean, and generally so compact when kept moist by the gentle surf that the inhabitants prefer the beach to the Neck Road while passing between the Neck and the Harbor with buggies. Unless the beach has been greatly disturbed by a storm its descent is gradual, but not so much so as to make a long wade necessary to obtain suitable depth. Here the elements combine their efforts to afford a luxury and a vigor that cannot be obtained in the cities. Here fashion drops her ornaments and seeks nature's health-giving freedom. Here the most delicate may experience the truth of the saying, ——

"On smoother beaches no sea birds light,
No blue waves shatter to foam more white."

And the thousands who have enjoyed the amusing incidents of the Beach among the temporary Mermen and Mermaids have found the social element to combine with those of the sea and air to fulfil the promise of the poet, —

"And the pale health-seeker findeth there
The wine of life in its pleasant air."

The Bathing Beach is on the east shore, and is distinguished by its many little houses seen from approaching steamers. It is near enough to the hotels, for going and coming, either on foot by the vigorous, or in carriages by others, is a necessary part of the enjoyment, giving a previous and subsequent circulation of the blood quite essential to health. Facilities for bathing are increasing annually, such as conveyances, suits, houses, etc. Up to the present time this beach has been remarkably free from accidents, and this may be owing in part to the required depth being found near the shore, and thus keeping the bathers from the greater force of the undertow, also keeping them nearer together.

In the vicinity of the bathing houses Mr. G. McCotter, from Brooklyn, has an interesting process of separating the black or iron sand from the other sand. This is done by magnetic attraction. The iron sand is used for the manufacture of steel, and large quantities are exported to New York.

THE PONDS.

These are among the remarkable features of Block Island. While thousands of tracts of land, high and low, uneven and level, may be found without lake or pond — each of these tracts larger than the Island, here a hundred may be counted that do not become dry once in ten years, none of them connected with a stream large enough to be called a brook. They are of all sizes and shapes, from the little duck pool to the great pond which is said to cover one thousand acres. They are of incalculable value to the little farms into which the land is divided, nearly, if not quite all of which are thus favored. Only the more important of these can here be described. The principal ponds are stocked with bass, and fine ones have been caught.

THE GREAT POND.

This, like the Island itself, has had various names. But the one most appropriate is the one here given. It is the oldest, and is probably the English of the Indian name given it by the Manisseans "time out of mind." This, too, is the name applied to it by Roger Williams, the noted Indian interpreter, in 1649. There is no good reason now for calling it "Salt," for it is *fresh*, too fresh for clams, scallops, and oysters. Many years ago it was properly a gulf, when it was connected with the ocean at the Breach.

Its depth is variable, and its bottom is uneven, like the surface of the Island in general. Twelve fathoms are its maximum on the side nearest the sea, from which it is separated by a narrow rim of sand, especially as seen from Beacon Hill. It abounds with fish which furnish sport to visitors who prefer its quiet surface to that of the rolling sea. It is a large and beautiful sheet of water, and very attractive to pleasure seekers who are fond of fishing, swimming, rowing, and sailing. Free from the swells and dangerous surf of the sea, several miles in length, and wide enough for long tacking in any wind, it will doubtless continue to increase in attractiveness. Besides, it is a study for the naturalist, for whence is its supply? If from the surrounding ocean, why is it fresh? Perhaps it illustrates Bacon's saying that "sea-water passing or straining through the sands leaveth the saltness."

How visited. From the harbor there are two routes. One is by Main Street to the Center. There turn to the right, pass the Littlefield Wind Mill, the Cemetery, and this is near the Great Pond. The other route is to leave Center Street at the Woonsocket House, turning to the right, and passing down the Neck Road, until Cemetery Street is intersected, where the Great Pond is soon reached, and the carriage may be driven along its water's edge, at the foot of Indian-Head-Neck, or it may follow the carriage way over Indian-Head-Neck towards the Cemetery, thence to the Center, and thence to the Harbor, making a pleasant hour's drive.

CHAGUM POND.

This is next in size to the Great Pond. Its name is commonly pronounced *Shawgum*, and it probably originated from an Indian who lived on the Island in 1711, was then a slave to some lordly master, stole a boat, ran away, lost the boat, was captured, and was punished by the wardens by six months added to his former period of servitude. Part of the Pond is in Sandy Point. Its water is fresh and clear, and on its northerly side is separated by a narrow Isthmus from the sea, over which the sea has been known to break into the pond, as it did in the great gale of 1815, passing over so deep, so suddenly, and with such force as to carry a footman, Edward Gorton, then passing, into the pond where he was buried so deep in the sand as never to be recovered. This pond is visited by the Neck Road, which leads to the Sandy Point Light House located near this pond.

THE FRESH POND.

It covers several acres, is free from the brackish taste of other ponds, is clear, and abundant in perch, and bass have been caught in it. Here visitors enjoy the game of "high hook," as the one is proclaimed who catches the most, and also the luxury of bathing. Near the shores of this pond, more than a century ago, was the central place of business, east of the north end. Here stood the first school-house, the first church, the parsonage, and the Honeywell Wind Mill.

This pond is reached by passing from the Harbor to the Center, and thence south about a mile. A short distance south or west of the pond visitors have fine views of the Atlantic, and of Montauk, by the aid of glasses.

SANDS POND.

This gem in an emerald setting is a curiosity as well as a thing of beauty. Its location is on some of the highest land of the Island, and has no watershed of any account, and neither inlet nor outlet now known. It is the clearest, and most regular shaped, has but a few feet of average depth, and never becomes dry. It is not easy to explain why a pond is there any more than in a thousand other places. No volcanic appearances suggest that it is an extinct crater with an invisible connection with some source of supply more elevated. This pond ought to furnish much of the ice of the Island. It takes its name from Dea. R. T. Sands and his brother William C. Sands who live near, and own land around its shores. In it are bass.

Visitors find the Sands Pond by passing from the Harbor up High Street to its junction with Dodge Street bearing to the right, and Dodge Street, passing Noah Dodge's fine residence, from which one of the best landscape views of the Island is had, leads to the Sands Pond. Thence, by cart track passing through a few gates, visitors may enter Center Street, near Fresh Pond, and thence enjoy good roads and fine prospects by the Center back to the Harbor.

THE MIDDLE POND.

This is on the Neck, near the west shore, south of Chagum Pond a short distance, and about midway between that and Wash Pond, a small body of water a little south of Middle Pond, and named as it is because around its shores, during the war of 1812 with England the British vessels often anchored near, and the marines came ashore there and washed their garments. At the middle pond they replenished their ships with fresh water — made fresh evidently by filtering from the sea through the sand. Here the Islanders bartered with the sailors, but were not allowed to sell rum, although they did it sometimes on the sly. Benjamin Sprague, now about ninety, says he was on his way there with barter, and met some English officers coming in elegant uniform on horses towards the Harbor. One said to Mr. Sprague "What have you to sell?" "Ducks, chickens, and beans," was the reply. "What's in that jug?" said the officer. Instead of answering, Mr. Sprague says,— "I looked him up in the face. He laughed, and said, 'I'll buy your ducks, chickens, and beans, and go on, and let my steward have them, and let my men have a drink apiece, but don't let them get drunk.' They went on, and so did I. Now, said I, there's good sailing, and I'll make a good voyage. So when I arrived at the Middle Pond the steward paid me for my ducks, etc., and I told him about the rum, and he nodded assent. I then went near the marines, put up two fingers, and beckoned them to follow me. I went down by the bank, behind some willows, and two came. The rum was half water, and I sold each a pint for a dollar a pint. After they went back two more came, and so on until I sold all out to them at a dollar a pint. As it was then about noon they urged me to dine with them, and I did, and they had their English rum with their rations. They asked me to drink some, and I did; and they asked me if I did not think their rum was better than mine. I told them, yes, but did not tell them how much of mine was water." By watering it he obeyed the commander's order — "Don't let any of them get drunk." Middle Pond will long be remembered as a favorite rendezvous for the English fleet in 1812. It is visited only by cart paths from the Neck Road.

THE HARBOR POND.

A little at the north of the Woonsocket House, and at the left while passing from the Harbor down the Neck Road, lies this body of brackish water, made so by its nearness to the Bay, and by the great amount of black or iron sand in its vicinity. At times its appearance is very rusty, and sometimes has a purple tinge. Its row boats, sailing boats, and fishing afford much pleasure. It is connected with Indian Head Pond, and the latter with Trimm's Pond.

TRIMM'S POND.

This pond takes its name from Godfrey Trimm who used to live on its west shore near Wm. P. Ball's, and at that house the woman almost gave a refugee "his quietus" with her scissors. In it is Ford Island, a little south of the southern extremity of the Great Pond. This pond straggles around more than any other, and does much to beautify the location of the Seaside House, and the landscape in front of the Central House, stretching from near the Neck Road to Cemetery Street. Its waters for many years have been noted for eel-fishing in winter, and as the home of the Island "Sea-serpent." He is so large that when seen a few years since by a sturdy young man, the latter hastened to the nearest house, trembling with fear, and tried to describe the "old settler." He was seen during the summer of 1876. The serpent is evidently a very large water-snake, harmless, and as shy as the ancient natives who, perhaps, worshiped this one's forefathers. The part of this pond east of Indian-Head-Neck is sometimes called *Indian Head Pond*.

THE MILL POND.

This is the only one of the kind on the Island, and is seen at the bridge between the Harbor and the Center. Here a mill for grinding corn anciently stood, and was built by Capt. James Sands. Here his only child at the time, "a girl just able to run about and prattle a little," was drowned. Here, too, was the "Sands Garrison," and an old, miniature earth-work still remains across the street from the pond. Here, since the memory of the present older generation, was also a "carding machine" for making "rolls" of wool. It is fed by a rill from a swamp southwest of the pond. It is a pleasant border to the schoolhouse lot near the pond, and a great convenience to Mr. Almanzo Littlefield.

THE SPRINGS.

The most noted springs of the Island are near the shore, southeasterly from the spring house to which their water is forced by a hydraulic ram. They boil up from the ground beautifully, and are a favorite resort, as they are furnished with cups, insulated, and surrounded by seats by Mr. B. B. Mitchell their owner, and the proprietor of the Spring House. They are found by a short stroll from the Breakwater southerly along the beach until one reaches the rill from them descending to the ocean. A few steps up this rill in a gentle gulley bring one to the springs. Or they may be reached by way of Spring Street and the Spring House. One is clear, cold, and palatable; the other is strongly impregnated with iron.

PLEASURE FISHING.

This is of comparatively recent origin on Block Island, and is an institution established and maintained entirely by visitors. For what Islander ever thought of catching a fish simply for the fun of it? Money or hunger has always been his motive for fishing. So while he enjoys his outlays for yacht, finely furnished for capturing the gamy blue fish and his neighboring denizens, supplying "gear" of all needed varieties, all in hope of revenue, the parties whom he serves enjoy the lively ocean sails about the Island, the graceful rocking of the vessel at anchor, while men are baiting hooks for gentler hands which have been thrilled there perhaps for the first time by a modest shake of a new acquaintance at the lower end of the line. The skipper thinks of his pay, and of the little accommodations he can afford to win the patronage of a second, and future voyages of the same gay party who seem to be as free with their money as with their jokes, laughter, and merriment of various descriptions. Now and then the heads of parties seem surprised to find that the sober Islander has learned and practices some of the tricks of business so common on the main land, and they wisely conclude that next time they will have a definite understanding before going aboard. This is an important prerequisite to a pleasant sailing party, preventing a temptation to the skipper, and also an unpleasant settlement, in some cases. The amount of pleasure, however, experienced by such excursionists depends mainly upon their own dispositions. If they expect that fisherman's yacht to be furnished with all the appointments of an elegant home or hotel ; if they expect to be free from the unavoidable color imparted by the sun and sea breeze; if they cannot endure the necessary fish odor that so much heightens by contrast the value of perfumery ; if they cannot pleasantly accept a little dash of spray over the bow occasionally ; if their clothing is too good to be soiled a little ; if they are too stiff necked to avoid the shifting boom, and thus get their hats, if not their heads smashed ; if they have no patience to endure the brief calm that deprives them of their dinner or tea ; if they are so unjust as to complain when no one is to blame ; if they have no sense of the ludicrous, and no skill for entertaining themselves and others they may be a party, but not a *pleasure* party while sailing and fishing together. Pleasure fishing, therefore, for its highest enjoyment at Block Island, requires a pleasant party, all of whom expect and prepare for inconveniences, expecting to "rough it" for a few hours, unanimously resolved to neither give nor take offence, but to assist each other in deriving all the amusement possible from the little voyage at sea with hook and line and bait for a little practice in "hauling."

The Pond Fishing is rapidly increasing in popularity. Here is less exposure to sea-sickness. Here a depth of water can be chosen that would afford no excuse for drowning, and at the same time the pleasures of boating and fishing can be enjoyed. Here the women and children can participate in safety, and it would require volumes to describe the amusements of pond fishing where fond parents watch the excitement among the boys and girls hauling the shiny perch in rapid succession. The happy days of childhood while fishing on the ponds of Block Island will form many bright and pictured pages in the memory of many in old age as they shall look back upon their excursions to, and summer life on the "little isle of the sea." Nor will the novelty and relish of eating the fish of their own catching be soon forgotten, and in the more sober thoughtfulness of riper years it will be better understood that these innumerable fishes were given us, not to school us in cruel insensibility, but "richly to enjoy." This is indicated even by the *silence* of the fish when captured. Were he to utter a cry of distress, like a rat in a steel-trap, or a pig in the hands of its owner — if a hundred fish in the boat were to do this at the same time we can imagine how great would be the temptation of sensitive persons to jump overboard. But as it is, all is pleasurable. The love of fishing is to be gratified on the same principle of gratifying the love of seeing. Light is for the eye, and so are fish for the fishermen.

Pond-fishing, like that in the yacht upon the sea, must be free from the etiquette of the drawing-room, in some respects, to have it pleasant. Too strict a regard for one's toilet can spoil all the amusement of the boat and tackle. Clothing should be worn that creates no painful anxiety about its being soiled or torn. If the feet, hands, and arms get wet — if the face is browned in the sun and wind, this is a part of the business and should occasion no fretting, but rather innocent jokes and laughter. Persons whose habit, or pleasure is that of spoiling the pleasures of others should never find a place in the party fishing for pleasure. A good rule to act upon at Block Island is, ——

"Let us laugh when we may, be sober when we can,
But vindicate the ways of God to man."

SURROUNDING WATERS.

Block Island Sound is the name applied by the U. S. Coast Survey to the body of water lying north of the Island, and separating it from the Charlestown and Watch Hill vicinity, and also approaching Point Judith. The narrowest place in this Sound, opposite Sandy Point, is a little less than ten miles in width.

Cow Cove, north of Chaguni Pond, was once much more distinct than at the present. Then Grove Point projected much farther, but like Sandy Point has been worn away by the heavy seas, until but little appearance of a bay remains. According to tradition the first settlers landed at Cow Cove, which is said to have taken its name from the fact that there they put overboard the first cow ever upon the Island, and in presence of the excited Indians compelled her to swim ashore.

Briton's Rock designates the water off Clay Head where a very dangerous rock is concealed in deep water, the top of which rises nearly to the surface. One of the most serious accidents in the history of the Islanders occurred there on the 9th of February, 1797. Gideon and John Rose, brothers, Samuel Wright and John Wills, while in their boat laden with perch for New York, were passing Clay Head in a fair southerly wind, and are supposed to have struck upon Briton's Rock, for they were there all drowned, and by a change of wind were all driven on shore and buried by their friends.

A similar calamity to the Island occurred on the night of Feb. 18, 1880. Then Captain Archibald Millikin, commander of a three-mast coaster, Captain George Addison Rose, and Elihu W. Rose, were drowned in Providence River between Fox Point and Mill Harbor. They were in a small yawl boat, the night was dark and windy, and they are supposed to have been capsized. Their bodies were recovered and buried by their many mourning friends.

Block Island Bay is the body of water making almost a semicircle of the shore from Clay Head to the Breakwater. It has the finest beach upon the Island, and in its waters all manner of vessels anchor with safety, except when the wind comes into the northeast. Then there is danger of being land-locked, or of going ashore. This bay affords a beautiful view, as seen from the prominent points along the eastern shore south of the harbor.

Old Harbor is opposite a section of the eastern shore extending from the Breakwater to Old Harbor Point. Many years ago, before the Pole Harbor was made, it was a place of frequent landing in fair weather. In that harbor was the origin of the "Harbor Boys" legend, as related in the account of the Refugees, and one of their ghosts reappeared not many years since, as an old Islander was near the springs of the Spring House, and listened with trembling to the solemn voice which was a little more grum than in his younger days. It was the first time he ever heard a hydraulic ram, and little imagined that his "Harbor Boy" was carrying water up to that hotel.

The Atlantic Ocean is the designation for the water from Old Harbor along the eastern shore to the south shore, and thence to Sandy Point.

The Breach, which was once of so great importance to the Island, does not now properly exist. At no time, now, does it connect the Great Pond with the sea, except by mechanical labor to reduce the high water in the Great Pond, and this is done by the town to keep the Neck Road passable. The easterly storms sometimes drive the heavy seas from the Block Island Bay over into the Great Pond, and when this occurs in connection with spring rains and thaws the Neck Road becomes impassable until the Breach is opened.

During those storms of high water innumerable fish in the Great Pond have escaped into the ocean, and thousands

THE BLOCK ISLAND BAY.

have been left on the sand between the Great Pond and the Bay, as the water has suddenly receded.

GRACE'S COVE.

This is on the west side of the Island, and is formed by a small projection of land into the sea, and this projection is known as Grace's Point. The Cove is not far from Sandy Hill, and has long been a place for landing small boats. Here the Mohegans landed, it is supposed, when they came, many centuries ago, from Stonington or Watch Hill to invade the Island by moonlight and were overpowered and starved on the Mohegan Bluffs. Here the brig Moluncus came ashore in 1855, and while her captain and crew were ashore bantering with wreckers she was got off by wind and tide in the night, and in the stormy night found by the wreckers.

DORRY'S COVE.

This also is on the west side, and probably took its name from Tormot Rose who was also called Dormot, and from Dormot came Dorry, and the cove was named after him either because he owned the land adjacent, or because of an incident which there occurred. The bank was precipitous many years ago, when he lived there, and he was clearing his land of stones by carting them with his oxen to the bank of the cove where he dumped them down into the sea. One day while backing his oxen for a dump he backed them too far and the cart loaded with stones went over the bank and took the oxen over too, and one was lost thereby. Mr. Rose mourned his loss so much that a neighbor said to him, — "Why, you mourn for your ox more than Job did for the loss of all of his." The afflicted man replied, — "Well, Job never had so likely an ox." The Cove is at the western terminus of Main Street.

II.

AN ABRIDGED HISTORY

OF

BLOCK ISLAND

FROM

1524 TO 1882.

BY

REV. S. T. LIVERMORE, A.M.

LOCATION.

Block Island is located directly south of the central point on the southern coast of Rhode Island, twelve miles out at sea, connected with the main land by a submerged bar well known to navigators. It is southwest from Newport about twenty-five miles, and about eighteen miles north of east from Montauk, which is the east end of Long Island. By the Coast survey its position is in latitude 41° 08' north, longitude 71° 33' west. It is sufficiently remote from the main shore, and small enough to be wholly exempt from the sultry land breezes of summer when its refreshing coolness is most enjoyable.

DISCOVERY.

When this Island was first discovered by the civilized world no one can state with certainty. Its first inhabitants known were a branch of the Narragansett Indians. The earliest record known of its discovery was in 1524, by Verrazano, a French navigator. He made a record of its location as being about fifty leagues east of New York, and three leagues from the main land, and described its shape as triangular, "full of hills, covered with trees."

Ninety years afterward the Island was visited by Adrian Block, a Dutch explorer, whose name is supposed to have been given to it by his crew, or by himself. They were probably the first civilized men who landed upon its shores. Their French predecessors seem to have sailed about it, as their account of it speaks of their having seen "fires all along the coast" of the Island.

In 1636 Captain John Oldham, a trader from Boston, visited the Island where he lost his life by the savages who, the ancient record says, "came into his boat, and having got a full view of commodities which gave them good content consulted how they might destroy him and his company, to the end they might clothe their bloody flesh with his lawful garments." By his death the Island became extensively known throughout New England and Europe.

ITS POSSESSION.

1. By the Aborigines. 2. By Massachusetts. 3. By four men. 4. By the first settlers and their descendants.

Its first owners of whom we have any account were the Narragansett Indians, and as they were a powerful tribe, occupying the main land nearest to the Island, we may suppose them to have held it for centuries previous to its discovery. Soon after the murder of Oldham it was subjugated by Colonel Endicott, under authority from Massachusetts, as a punishment for that murder, and its possession by that colony was acknowledged to Governor Vane in 1637 by the Chief Miantinomo, the great Sachem of the Narragansetts. Of this transfer Governor Winthrop said in 1637, — "Miantinomo, the Narragansett Sachem, came to Boston. The governor, deputy, and treasurer treated with him, and they parted upon fair terms. He acknowledged that all the Pequod country and Block Island were ours, and promised that he would not meddle with them but by our leave." But what had that chief to do with the *Pequod* country? Roger Williams was intimately acquainted with the natives of Block Island before it was settled by the English, and in 1637 wrote to Governor Winthrop that they had obligated themselves to pay a tax to Massachusetts, and its subjects, of one hundred fathoms of beads or wampum annually. In 1658 the Island was transferred from said colony to John Endicott, Richard Bellingham, Daniel Dennison, and William Hawthorne, and in 1660 they sold it to sixteen individuals for £400, and these last purchasers had the Island surveyed and apportioned to each buyer in 1661, and in 1662, with their families, their sailing vessels built at Braintree, near Boston, having been sailed around Cape Cod to Taunton to meet the emigrants, there embarked, passed down the Taunton River, and thence to the Island where they and their descendants have since remained and prospered.

ITS NAMES.

Manisses was its original and Indian name, signifying "Little God," or "Little God's Island." This also was the name of its first inhabitants of whom we have any knowledge. Its origin and first application to the Island will ever remain one of the hidden mysteries of the Aborigines.

Claudia was its first civilized name, given to it by Verrazzano in 1524 in honor of the mother of Francis I, king of France.

Adrian's England was the name put upon the Dutch maps in 1614. This is essentially the same as the name now in use, and was modified by the colonists to

Block Island. This name continued in use, unaltered by its English occupants and others until 1672, and will probably never be supplanted, unless the more euphonic and ancient *Manisses* shall be resumed.

New Shoreham, alias *Block Island,* was the name incorporated into the town charter of the Island in 1672, and for about two hundred years this prefix had the monopoly. It was adopted in said charter as a reminder of places in England dear to the memory of the Islanders, or as they expressed it — " As signs of our unity and likeness to many parts of our native country." The final syllable *ham,* meaning *house, farm,* or *village,* is very common in England.

The Ministerial Lands is another name of the Island that was somewhat common anciently, and is very significant of the character of the little colony there who, when they surveyed the land for themselves in 1661, also apportioned a part for the support of the gospel among them, and that land they said should *"continue for that use for ever."*

Block-house Island, on an old map in the State Library at

Albany, printed in Augsburg in 1777, originated from the "topographical observations of C. J. Southier," and he probably imagined its origin to be from that kind of a house then common in the colonies, and upon his own authority appended the word *house*.

The last modification of this name has been the recent change in the Post Office Department where it is now simply *Block Island*.

ITS SURFACE AND PRODUCTS.

"It was full of hills," was the French navigator's description in 1524, and none better, perhaps, can be given. A more uneven surface but few, if any, have ever seen. It will be very difficult to find its equal, except as one looks at the ocean when its surface is covered with one tidal wave followed by another, on and between both of which are innumerable regular and chop waves of all dimensions. Between these little hills are hundreds of ponds, while the Great Pond in relation to the Island is an inland sea. The multitude of walls which now fence the little farms there indicate the inconvenience of cultivating the soil by the early settlers. No ledges there have yet been discovered, but granite boulders and pebbles without number, in a soil naturally quick and productive.

Three and a half centuries ago the Island was "covered with trees." When taken from the Indians in 1637 it was well timbered and had two large cornfields protected on all sides by forests. One of these was on the southerly part, and the other on the northerly part known by the early settlers as the "Corne Neck," and now called *The Neck*. The first settlers for sixty years had timber sufficient for buildings, fences, and fuel, but peat was almost the only material for "firing" from 1760 to 1860, and it is still abundant in many of nature's pockets between the hills of the Island, while of but few can it now be said, —

> "Old wives spinning their webs of tow,
> Or rocking weirdly to and fro
> In and out of the *peat's* dull glow."

The products of the Island during the last hundred years have not been sufficient to give support and thrift to its dense population, although its soil has been well nourished with fish offal and about 10,000 loads of sea-weed annually. Its noted fisheries have ever been a principal support and source of revenue to its inhabitants, who have found a ready market in many cities along the neighboring coast, until its attractiveness as a summer resort has created a large home demand in the watering season. A detailed account of its resources — grain, fish, sea-moss, poultry, eggs, etc., may be seen in its history published in 1877.

THE INHABITANTS.

They are of English descent, of the Roger Williams stamp, and have maintained their identity as a colony with remarkable tenacity. In 1877 their population was 1,147; 1,138 of whom were American born, and 1,032 were born upon the Island. Where is there another such a locality? The men are hardy, industrious, and brave sailors. They live better than the average of country people. In 1877 there were 110 in 619 adults who were over 60 years old.

Intellectually the men are in advance of those in country towns generally. Their trading excursions along the main coast from Portland to New York have given them good opportunities for observing men and things, and in latter years much of the outside world in various phases has come to them in pursuit of health and pleasure. They are all skilled in the art of driving a good bargain, and have the faculty of keeping what they have gained, which with their industry makes them a very independent people. They are rapidly improving in educational interests, as evinced by their new and well appointed school houses. They are far more courageous as sailors than otherwise. They have never had a jail nor a resident lawyer. Chief Warden Wm. P. Lewis, in 1877 had tried 100 cases, 80 civil, 20 criminal, without a lawyer except in one case, and then he was defeated.

The Women of the Island have been noted for their in dusty and devotion to the domestic relations. Vigorous, virtuous, dignified and genial, they have heartily coöperated with the men in obtaining a livelihood, and in promoting the welfare of society. Tidy, but not gaudy; frank, but never simpering, what they have lacked in refined education has been compensated for by a large supply of common sense and native genius. Some of them have well improved their advantages in schools abroad, and the boys and girls of the rising generation are obtaining a degree of intelligence and refinement quite in advance of former generations.

The morals of the Islanders will compare favorably with any other locality of equal population. Their self imposed taxes for educational and religious purposes have been considerably heavier than the average of such taxes on the main land. Indeed, the first settlers were distinguished by their intelligence and good morals, and as such attracted the attention of Benjamin Franklin, Major-General Greene, and others of distinction. The wife of Simon Ray, jr., was the granddaughter of Roger Williams, and this Mr. Ray and his father were the resident, unordained ministers of the Island ninety years. Anna Ray married Governor Samuel Ward of Rhode Island, and her sister Catharine married Governor William Greene, of the same state, and as they had no brothers their family disappeared, but their good influence has been perpetuated with the surname *Ray*, so common among the Islanders, until the present. Much might be said, too, of the moral power of James

Sands, a leading man among the first settlers whose descendants are still upon the Island, and much respected.

HOSTILITIES.

Casual visitors there little imagine the hostile scenes that have been enacted where they now see only the signs of peace and pleasure. More detailed accounts of them may be found in the History of Block Island than can here be given. The rich cornfields three centuries ago, the ample fishing grounds on and around the Island, the abundance of fowls there, especially those migrating in spring and fall, and the exhaustless stores of scallops and oysters then in the Great Pond, made the ancient *Manisses* a tempting bone of contention between the Narragansetts, Mohegans, and Pequots. The natives used to relate to the early settlers strange and bloody conflicts between these hostile tribes. At one time the Island Indians, many centuries ago, started on an expedition, in their canoes, against the Mohegans forty miles distant, on the main land. At the same time, by moonlight, the Mohegans launched their fleet of canoes for the Island, but were first discovered by the Islanders who had the reflection of the light in their favor, and they therefore put back, hauled their canoes ashore and hid them, and then lay in ambush for the Mohegans who landed, marched into the interior while their canoes were smashed, and their retreat was cut off by the Islanders who pursued the invaders, drove them to the Mohegan Bluffs, so named from this affair, and there hemmed them in until they perished from starvation. At that point in 1760, was an earth-work called the Mohegan Fort, and unless it has sloughed off into the sea by the action of frost and tides a relic of it may yet be discovered. The savage appearance of the warriors whose wigwams once occupied the places where hotels and private residences are now standing is indicated by a Mr. Vincent who, centuries ago, described the Pequots as

"Straight and tall, of limbs big and strong, seldom seen violent or extreme in any passion. Naked they go, except a skin about their waist, and sometimes a mantle about their shoulders. Armed they are with bows and arrows, clubs, javelins, etc."

Besides the savage wars among the Indians themselves, new hostilities occurred between them and the English soon after the settlement of the colonies. In 1636 the Indians murdered Captain John Oldham near Sandy Point, in his vessel, for which barbarity the savages were severely punished by Massachusetts soon after by the invasion of Col. John Endicott, whose little fleet bore to their shores the first firearms known upon the Island. The expedition was twofold, to "do justice unto the Indians for the murder of Mr. Oldham," and to seize and hold the Island by right of conquest. After the little army had been absent from Boston six weeks one of its soldiers, Israel Stoughton, wrote back to a friend, — "We are now ready for Block Island, only we wait for a fair wind. We are informed of many Indians there, so we expect the toughest work we have had yet." The fair N. E. wind came and bore away their fleet to its destination along the bathing beach of the Island where they anchored, and found much difficulty in wading ashore on account of the surf. Endicott's men were met by a volley of arrows from about forty Indians who quickly fled when they heard the volley of muskets and saw their deadly effects. The invaders burned about sixty wigwams, "their mats, and some corn, and staved seven canoes, and departed," doubtless with a good supply of plunder. The conquest, however, was not completed until a second expedition under the above-named Stoughton in 1637, who landed his forces there in the night, killed a few of the natives, burnt a few wigwams, "came to parley," made a treaty of subjugation by which the Indians were to pay a tribute of "one hundred fathom of wampum peague" [beads] to

Massachusetts annually. This treaty became void when the Island passed into the possession of the little colony by whose descendants it is now occupied.

The second, and last hostile demonstrations on the Island, in which the Indians were a party, was within a few years after its settlement. Conscious of their greater numbers and power, the sixteen families were looked upon as intruders, far away from allies, and a constant temptation to the flint arrow, the tomahawk, and the scalping knife. Moreover, traders sold firearms and *fire-water* to the Indians, and thus imperiled the infant colony. Individual collisions occurred. Precautions were taken by the settlers. They established a little garrison, threw up an earth-work still to be seen near the bridge on the road from the Harbor to the Center. They had a counsel of war, and decided that their safety depended upon their bravery and fearless appearance. By mustering in all their forces they raised an army of sixteen men and a boy. Thomas Terry, then one of the proprietors, full of the military spirit, and the ancestor of the many Terrys since then distinguished for their bravery, and others agreed to challenge all the Indian warriors on the Island to a pitched battle. This was done, the challenge accepted, the day fixed, and preparations made for the fight. The day came, and with it thirty strange Indians from the main land with new guns. Terry, in the morning, met them as they came from the east shore near Clay Head towards Indian-Head-Neck. He halted them, questioned them closely, forbade their advance, disarmed them one by one, put their guns into his house near by until they should return, made them sit down until he had passed the fort on Fort Island where the Indians had assembled for the battle. To that Fort the strange Indians were then welcomed with the most savage yells of applause. But the little army of seventeen, undaunted marched boldly within arrow shot of the Fort, led by the music of a single drum briskly played by a Mr. Kent, (who afterwards moved to Swansea), and there they repeated their challenge, but no enemy came out to fight, the hand of peace was shaken, and both parties were friendly thereafter. (See detailed account in History, under "Thomas Terry.")

THE FRENCH.

The French Hostilities, about the year 1690, were very damaging to Block Island. At that time France and England were at war, and to fight the New England colonies then was to fight England, and the position of the Island was favorable to the enemy, and its commodities of grain, cattle, and poultry were tempting to the French privateers. In Newport the approach of the enemy was "proclaimed by beat of drum," and the threatened danger from abroad, added to that of perils from the natives at home, caused a tax on the Island, in May, 1690, of £17 10s. "for the support of their majesty's interest against the French and Indian enemies."

William Trimming's invasion for plunder was very disastrous to the Island. In July, 1689, he entered the Bay with "a large bark, a barge, a large sloop, and a lesser one," and by his fluent English made the armed Islanders believe that he was George Austin, a noted English privateer. Under this deception he landed his marines, whose guns were concealed in their boats until they reached the shore, when they suddenly attacked and obtained control of the Island. The captured soldiers were imprisoned in Captain James Sand's stone house, and their guns were broken to pieces on the rocks by the French, and a general pillage of the Island followed, killing cattle for food, and also to impoverish the inhabitants, one of whom made this record,—"They continued about a week on the Island, plundering houses, stripping the people of their clothing, ripping up beds, throwing out the feathers, and carrying away the ticking." A Frenchman insulted the wife of the Quaker physician, Dr. John Rodman, then described as "a very desirable gentlewoman." The Quaker sprang between them, the ruffian cocked his pistol at him, while the latter bared his bosom and deliberately said,—"Thee may do it if thou pleasest, but thou shalt not abuse my wife."

This invasion aroused the colonies, and men-of-war from Boston and New York were sent to the rescue. The hostile fleet was scattered, a part of it captured, and the perfidious Trimming was killed on Fisher's Island.

A second visit from the French before the close of the year 1689 occurred in the night, with consequences similar to the former, but probably more terrifying to the inhabitants. One of them, many years afterwards known as the venerable Samuel Niles of Braintree, Mass., then suffered in person more than any other, of which he says,—"I suppose I was the greatest sufferer of any under their hands at that time; for before I had dressed myself one of their company rushed into the chamber where I lodged. Being alone, without any of his company, not knowing what dangers might befal him, on a sudden, and with a different air, he says to me, 'Go down, you dog.' To which I replied, 'Presently, as soon as I have put on my stockings and shoes.' At which, with the muzzle of his gun he gave me a violent thrust at the pit of my stomach, that it threw me back on the bed, as I was sitting on the bed-side, so that it was some time before I could recover my breath. He drew his cutlass and beat me, smiting me with all his power, to the head of the stairs, and it was a very large chamber. He followed me down the stairs, and then bound my hands behind me with a sharp, small line, which soon made my hands swell and become painful."

The Frenchman must have struck with the flat side of his cutlass, and probably hit where no bones were broken, or Mr. Niles would have described minutely the fracture.

A third hostile demonstration from the French occurred on Sunday, without any opposition. The inhabitants concealed themselves as best they could, some "betaking themselves to the woods for shelter." The stay of the enemy was short, as they soon saw the approach of the English man-of-war Nonesuch, under command of Capt. Dobbins. After they had hastened from the headquarters of the Island an eyewitness made this record,—"We went boldly (?) to the house, and found the floor covered with geese, with blood and feathers; the quarters of the hogs they had killed hanging up in one and another part of the house—a melancholy sight to behold! Their manner of dressing hogs after they had quartered them was to singe off the hair over a flame; and their method to command the cattle was (as I saw when they took us before) to thrust their cutlasses in at their loins, and on a sudden the hind quarter would drop down, and as the poor creature strove to go forward, the blood would spout out of the hole, and fly up near or full a yard in height."

These repeated invasions caused but little personal injury, while they were very damaging to property, and were very terrifying to all the Islanders. A *fourth* and similar demonstration was made upon this unprotected "isle of the sea," either by the French, or by pirates. They were bravely repulsed "in an open pitched battle, and driven off from the shore," while the victors escaped injury, "except one man slightly wounded in his finger." The battlefield was probably in the vicinity of the Harbor, as vessels usually anchored in the Bay.

During this hostile period of about twenty-five years the condition of the Islanders may be seen in their petition to the "*General Assembly of Rhode Island and Providence Plantations*," the first few lines of which are here given:— "The humble petition of the poor distressed Inhabitants of Block Island which expect daily No other than to be

Invaded, our houses demolished, our persons and Estates become a prey to the enemy If no other assistance can be had than what we can raise within ourselves." Twenty years now passed away without any special alarm, until the 18th of April, 1717, when a strange sloop of the largest class anchored in the Bay, and some of the crew came ashore, and then with fresh supplies returned peacefully to their vessels accompanied by the Islanders. This sloop, with some reason, may be supposed to have belonged to the pirate Captain Kidd. It was under command of one then named Williams. His conduct, like Kidd's, was a mixture of humanity and barbarism, for just before weighing anchor, after the boat containing the Islanders had gone from the sloop part way to the shore, they were compelled to go back to the sloop, and there three of their number, "George Mitchell, William Toesh, and Doctor James Sweete," were kidnapped by these pirates and what became of them is a mystery.

From the beginning of the seventeenth century to the Revolution of 1776 the Island enjoyed a good degree of peace and prosperity.

REVOLUTIONARY.

The Revolutionary Hostilities were by far the most damaging to the Island of any that have ever occurred. No braver resolutions were passed in the colonies than those which Block Island put upon her record at a town meeting held March 2, 1774. (See History, page 88.) No other place was exposed to greater dangers, and yet the patriotic Islanders put their property, lives, and sacred honor as patriotically upon their country's altar as did the signers of the Declaration of Independence. As the war-cloud thickened it enwrapped the little Island in two-fold darkness, as it was soon after more thoroughly sacked by the mother colony than it ever had been by the French privateers, and then was left by her to the cruel mercies of the approaching hostile ships of England. One hundred years it had been represented in her General Assembly, and had paid taxes into her treasury. One hundred years it had maintained good order, and some of its families stood in the first ranks of society, but now, when help and sympathy were most needed, none could be given.

In August, 1775, the Rhode Island Assembly passed an act that took from the Islanders all the cattle and sheep not then needed there for immediate subsistence, and enacted "that two hundred and fifty men be sent upon that Island to secure the stock until it can be brought off." About 2000 sheep and lambs were thus taken from their owners together with many cows and oxen. Many a tear, doubtless, was shed as these familiar animals, many of them pets of women and children, were taken away. In February of the next year, 1776, another act by the R. I. Assembly was passed to impoverish the Island still more by taking from it more sheep and cattle, and its firearms and all its military stores. Some compensation was allowed by the mother colony. While Joseph Dennison 2d was transporting in the schooner Folly the stock to the main all were captured by the British. About this time the colony sent Jonathan Hazard to the Island with instructions to "earnestly exhort the inhabitants to remove from the Island." This was soon followed by an act forbidding them to land on the Rhode Island coast, except to become citizens on the main, under penalty of fine and imprisonment, and all inhabitants of the State were empowered to arrest and lodge in jail any such intruder from the Island. Indeed, Block Island, at the beginning of the Revolution, loyal as it was to the cause of liberty, was first thoroughly sacked, and then virtually banished by its mother colony. This was the result of a military necessity, as it could not be protected by her, and as its resources left there would have been captured by the enemy, and the Island, as stated in the bill of excommunication, was "entirely in the power of the enemy." The fish-lines, and samp-mortars, hand cards, and spinning-wheels, were left to the Islanders. Cut off from groceries, from mechanic shops, from flour mills, from all markets, and left to the mercy of an enemy whose ships were constantly hovering around her shores, the little isolated colony braved the terrors of the situation as nobly as any band of Spartans found upon the pages of history. We have no record of a murmur from their lips against the mother colony, nor of an act that indicates a regret of their patriotic offering of their all upon the altar of liberty. But their situation, painful in the extreme, heroically endured, was too pitiful for endurance on the main land, and it awakened the deepest sympathies from the parent colony whose Assembly relaxed its stringency, and allowed, in 1777, a limited communication to be resumed. The last act of colonial severity towards the Island was in February, 1779, and that act fell upon the already scathed and isolated few like the crash of a thunderbolt, whose force was partially spent upon Waite Saunders, Thomas Carpenter, and Peleg Hoxie of Kings county of R. I., as they were arrested for "having carried on an illicit commerce with the inhabitants of New Shoreham," *i. e.* Block Island. Their conviction would of course implicate also the Islanders of whom "Wm. Gorton, Robert Champlin, John Cross, Samuel Taylor, Simon Littlefield, Joseph Sands, John Paine, Stephen Franklin, Edward Sands, and Robert Congdon," were summoned to appear immediately before the Assembly, "upon the penalty of £150, lawful money each, for non-appearance." Whether these principal men of the Island were convicted of participating in said "illicit commerce," or what the result of the investigation was we have not been able to ascertain. No doubt there were some upon the Island whose extremities made them yield to the temptations of British bribes, and for this reason, in one of its preambles, the General Assembly of Rhode Island made this record : — " Whereas, the said town of New Shoreham hath been for a long time, and still is, within the power and jurisdiction of the enemies of the United States, whereby they obtain, in consequence of the evil practices aforesaid, supplies for themselves, and intelligence from time to time of the situation of our troops, posts, and shores ; by which means they are enabled to make frequent incursions, and thereby commit devastations upon, and rob the innocent inhabitants of their property, and deprive them of their subsistence ; wherefore,

Be it enacted, etc." Suspicions were sharpened against the Islanders in September, 1779, when a British vessel was captured by an American privateer, and whom should our brave sailors find upon the decks of their prize but two Block Islanders — John Rose and Frederick Wyllis! They were arrested by the sheriff, delivered to Col. Christopher Greene, and by him passed over to Maj. Gen. Gates to be treated as prisoners of war. In May of 1779 Stephen Franklin, an Islander, was arraigned before the General Assembly for complicity with the British, and passed over to Gen. Gates to be tried as a spy.

REFUGEES.

In addition to the troubles from the mother colony and from the British during the revolution the Island was kept in almost constant alarm by a class of persons known as *Refugees*. They were deserters mainly from both armies, and were perfect desperadoes, going singly, or in bands, unprincipled and cruel in their demands. One of these outlaws entered a house in the vicinity of the Littlefield Wind-Mill. He was seen by the watchful inmates at a little distance. The husband hid up-stairs in a pile of flax. The refugee entered, and among his insolent inquiries said to the wife, — " Where is your husband ? " She answered sharply, "I haven't any!" She probably considered him divorced while concealed in the flax. A few more insolent inquiries banished her fears and filled her with indignation, and as he was about to break open a chest in the corner she seized her scissors, and flew at him with the pointed blade in position to stab, exclaiming in terrific tones, — "Get out of this house, you infernal villain, or I'll kill you with these scissors!" As he was not prepared for his "quietus with a bodkin," the next act in the almost tragic scene was — *Exit Refugee.*

At another time a whole band of refugees approached the house of John Sands. The inmates were terror stricken, the visit of the desperate creatures was so well understood. Here again the bravery of the Island women was demonstrated. Mrs. Sands comprehended the whole situation and instantly laid her plan of defence. She put her babe in the cradle, and did not wait for them to obtain admittance to her house, but made it her castle by holding it in her control, as she seized a gun, and with it promised in meaning terms the death of the first Refugee who might attempt to enter. Neither of them being willing to be shot thus they departed. Sometimes a band of these marauders would pass over from the main land to the Island in a light row boat that could elude the swiftest sails. A galley of these roughs, according to tradition, nine in number, four oarsmen on a side, and a helmsman, approached the Island for plunder. They attempted to land at the Old Harbor Landing, near the spring of the Spring House. They probably intended to land in the night. The burning flames of oil upon Beacon Hill are supposed to have signaled their approach in that kind of a boat then called a "Shaving Mill." But with the darkness of that evening came also a heavy sea from the southeast. The boat was now tossed to and fro like a shaving upon the waves. The armed Islanders inferred the intended point of landing, and there secreted themselves behind rocks and boulders to give the invaders a warm reception. But the darkness grew dense; the seas rolled higher as the wind increased; the surf dashed fearfully against the rocky shore; and only occasional dim views could be had of the " Shaving Mill," until nothing was visible upon sea or land, and nothing was heard amid the angry tones of the sea but the suppressed words passing from one to another on the alert for the enemy, until a strong determined voice upon the deep was heard thundering out the command — " Row ! boys, row for your lives ! " The *Refugees* were approaching the shore ! But as soon as they were near enough to be struck by the surf their " Shaving Mill " went to pieces, and the last ever known of them was their drowning cry — " Help ! Help ! " piercing the darkness, and reaching only the ears of those whom they intended to rob. From that ill-fated crew originated the weird legend of the " Harbor Boys," whom the Islanders for a hundred years supposed to be the ghosts of the drowned refugees still hovering about the Old Harbor landing, and repeating in dark stormy nights there the old command — " Row ! boys, row ! " and the cries — " Help ! Help ! " The writer has conversed with men who say they have heard these mysterious voices there, and these ghostly voices are spoken of by the old inhabitants as the " Harbor Boys." Why not imagine these ghosts to be the crew of the fire ship that used to glide about Sandy Point, and which some one named after the Palatine ?

When the storm cloud of the Revolution had passed over, nowhere were the sunshine and the bow of promise more welcome than on Block Island, and ever since then it has shared in the state counsels, and in the sympathy of the mother colony.

The war of 1812, instead of bringing hostility to the Island, brought double friendship and prosperity, as both hostile nations declared it to be neutral ground, and the

British there replenished their vessels with water and provisions and paid the gold liberally for these supplies, and by their good discipline and gentlemanly behavior left a pleasant impression upon the memories of the Islanders.

During the long struggle of the colonies for independence the inhabitants of Block Island, with no earthly ally, amenable to no other than its own civil authority, except as claimed by Great Britain to belong to its crown, enjoyed and enforced all the fundamental principles of a pure democracy. Whether familiar with any treatises of jurisprudence, like those of Justinian, Blackstone, or Vattel,— whether they had ever seen a code or not, they certainly had a clear knowledge of human rights and duties, and they put that knowledge into practice in a manner that would have been a model for the sages of Athens and for the writer of our Declaration of Independence. The town records of this little, forsaken, war-pillaged Island, then in sight and hearing of the wrathful guns booming on the main, show a love of freedom and a faith in its attainment and possession that were marvelous. The inhabitants drew up a constitution of their own, made their own laws, established their own civil tribunal for all grades of litigation, investing in their high court of three wardens the power of decision in all cases, except in trial for life, beyond which decision there was no appeal; and in trial for life the court consisted of said three wardens and six associate freeholders, and the decision of a majority of this tribunal was without appeal, and these associate freeholders were finable £20 each for absence from the trial for capital punishment. Thus the little model democracy, amidst the ravages of war, isolated, few in number, forsaken by its mother colony, and within reach of the paws of the growling British lion, and infested night and day by lawless Refugees, and even by the treachery of a few of its own citizens, all through the long years of the Revolution, had its regular elections, as though it were one of the powerful nations of the earth, maintained civil and religious order, attended to transfers of real estates, kept a record of marriages, births, and deaths, cared for the poor, assessed and collected taxes, but left no record of murmuring at their lot, or of doubt that under the leadership of Washington and Greene, the latter of whom married one of the daughters of the Island, would ultimately lead our brave armies to victory.

THE FISHERIES OF BLOCK ISLAND.

It would be very interesting to learn when the first fish was taken from the waters of Block Island, and to state the number of millions there captured. Such a history would probably take us back a thousand years or more. The old native Manisseans used to narrate their war legends to Samuel Niles, more than two centuries ago, and those legends may have come down from a period of many centuries before Niles conversed with those Indians. Those war legends indicate the great value placed upon the Island of Manisses, which means the *Little god Island*, as they were waged for its valuable fisheries, for there were plenty of other lands quite as valuable for corn. Then, too, the Breach into the Great Pond was providentially kept open, and immense quantities of oysters, scallops, and other shell-fish were there produced. Now, to produce the same a little enterprise is necessary. Indeed it is not twenty-five years since large quantities of oysters were raked from the bottom of the Great Pond.

The Indians also fished with lines similar, probably, to those upon which they strung their wampum. The sinkers to these lines indicate the large fish caught, and the deep water from which they were taken. They were stone, some of which are preserved, weighing from a half to two pounds, round, oblong, with a deep groove cut in each longitudinally around the center, and the line was tied around the sinker in its groove. We do not know what they used for hooks, but may suppose they combined a sharp tooth with a shank to which the line was fastened, as did the Sandwich Islanders, whose hooks we have.

The first record we find concerning the fishing business of the Island by the settlers was made in 1670, when, in response to a petition from the Islanders, the General Assembly of Rhode Island appointed a committee to raise contributions "to make a convenient harbor there, to the *encouradging fishing designs.*" This had reference to exportation of fish from the Island, and implies the beginning of the business that has been one of the principal supports of the Island. In 1675 an incident there occurred indicative of business and morals. Peter George, one of the first settlers, had a Negro by the name of Wrathy, who was publicly whipped with twelve lashes for "staling fish from Steven the Endian." The Negro was then *Wrathy* indeed, and *he*, at least, considered fish on Block Island very costly.

That the fisheries of the Island, one hundred and eighty years ago, had become a lucrative business is evident from the following record in the old town book, put there in April, 1702. The record, as follows, is instructive in several respects. "Then Capt. John Merritt brought before us one John Meeker for being a delinquent for absenting himself from out of said Merritt's employment, being his servant for the fishing season for forty shillings pr. month with six pounds of bread and six pounds of pork a week, the which considerations the said Meeker did promise to his faithful service till the middle of June or thereabouts as by witness on oath doth appear before us. We therefore determine and give our judgment that the said Meeker shall perform the said conditions as above said. The forty shillings pr. month is to be paid current money of the

Colony with cost of Court which is one shilling for the constable's fees, and two shillings for other charges which said Meeker is to pay.

"Given under our hands,
SIMON RAY, *Sen. Warden*,
EDWARD BALL, *Dep. Warden*."

During this same year, 1702, the fisheries were of sufficient extent to make the saving of oil quite a business, for then the town sold six barrels of "oyle for ammunition." Indeed, still farther back, in 1695, the town stipulated with one Robert Carr, an Islander, in reference to the Great Pond, to be "forward in making a harbor and promoting the *fishing trade*." In 1723 the Rhode Island Legislature took action in reference to the Block Island Fisheries which were then impeded "For the want of a pier at said Island, for the encouragement of the navigation of this Colony, *especially the fishery*, which is begun to be carried on successfully."

The seasons for the most profitable fishing are fall and spring. In November the inestimable droves of cod-fish travel southerly, and they seem to make Block Island one of their guide-posts, for the uniformity of their movements from century to century indicates their familiarity with the waymarks and "paths of the sea." They are known by fishermen as "deep water" or "bottom fish," on account of their swimming so near the bottom of the water. If diverted from their paths, and likely to be overtaken by a storm in too shallow water, they are sagacious enough to swallow smooth pebbles for more ballast, or to enable them to keep to the bottom to prevent them from being driven ashore. From this fact the fishermen have sometimes been warned of their own dangers, which are neither few nor small. Their success depends much upon their finding the paths of these deep water travelers, as they have parallel courses, and the men with hooks and lines "strike them" sometimes in one and sometimes in another. These paths are on all sides of the Island, on which so many millions of these deep water "crafts" have been wrecked that if it were possible for Neptune or others of the "codfish aristocracy" to obtain a hearing at Washington, a strong petition for the removal of Block Island would be pressed with great pathos and persistence. But this "aristocracy" will not learn wisdom from their disasters, and so each generation follows the paths of its predecessors. In the autumn the cod come much nearer to the Island than in spring, thus greatly favoring the fishermen by shortening their distance in the short days, and enabling them to return the more quickly to harbor on account of sudden storms, as at times they are obliged to weigh anchor, hoist sails, and fly, like a rising flock of birds, for safety.

The fishing is done in water from ten to twenty fathoms deep. Lines and hooks are used that are strong enough to "haul in" fifty pounds rapidly. The salt water is so penetrating and softening to the hands that a cot or glove to protect each forefinger is necessary. The line is hauled over the hard oak "gunnel," which is sometimes, when old, seen with deep cuts in it made by the lines while hauling the fish. "High-hook" is the title which is given to the one who has caught the most fish for the day. "Who is *high-hook* to-day?" is a common inquiry after thirty or forty Island boats have landed at the Harbor with their treasures.

After the fall fishing, and through much of the winter, there are a few smacksmen who continue fishing through the cold weather. Their vessels have decks, cabins, fires, berths, and cooking conveniences, although at night and during storms they take shelter within the Break-water. In the center of some of their smacks is a "well"—a place open from top to bottom admitting sea water equal in depth to the draught of the vessel, and in this water fish are kept alive, new water coming in at the bottom, and thus from a thousand to fifteen hundred in a vessel are taken to market, and while sailing all the fish in the well are headed in the direction in which the vessel is going, as though they were working their passage.

Trawl fishing has been carried on to some extent within the Island fisheries. This consists principally of fishing with about a thousand hooks set by a single crew. The hooks are attached to lines about two feet long, and each of these lines a few feet apart is fastened to a rope which is sunk at a certain point at sea, where a buoy is left to mark the spot, and this line is stretched, sunk, and buoyed so that it is near the bottom with its tempting clams for baits on the hooks. All the fish have to do then to be caught is to take the bait, fasten themselves on the hook, and be hauled up on the long rope and manipulated by the happy fisherman who rejoices in a full line.

The spring fishing is much like that in autumn. As the cod return northerly they keep farther from the Island, for the most part, than at other times. This may be owing to the direction given to them by the southerly shores of Long Island. They also seem to be more numerous in spring, owing, perhaps, to their being less scattered in different paths, which also may be narrower. These paths are generally called "banks" by the fishermen. They lie in spring from five to twenty miles from the Island. Many more are caught in the spring than in the autumn. The spring season extends from the first of April until into June. During this season the mild weather, the distance of the sail, the large number in the business, the early starting in the morning, the rapid footsteps along the streets from two o'clock until four in the morning, the rattle of sails hoisting in the harbor, the sailor phrases of the fishermen, and the anxious movements to become "high-hook" for the day, make up a scene of life and beauty that must be witnessed to be appreciated. It is then that Whittier's stanza comes in,—

> "When boats to their morning fishing go,
> And, held to the wind and slanting low,
> Whitening and darkening the small sails show."

It is a charming scene, in the month of May, to view from an elevated point on the land from thirty to fifty small sails going out to the Banks, as one of those narrow slumbering clouds skirts the eastern horizon, under which cloud the red sun begins to show himself rising out of the sea, and towards whom the vessels are gently moving in a long line stretching from the last one rounding the Breakwater to those apparently sailing into the face of the sun, whose rays have soon converted said cloud into a wreath of fretted gold for the brow of the king of day, while the stillness of the morning is broken only by the solemn murmur of wearied waves that finish their journey along the shore.

Far different is the scene in the afternoon when one after another of the same boats, from various points of the compass, come straggling back, as if working hard to bring their burdens that press the gunnels to the water, with wet and wearied fishermen who have thrown overboard tons of ballast stones to make room for the hungry and hunger-satisfying cod-fish, many of which Cooper's Leatherstocking would call "*sock-dolligers.*" Then follows the lively work of dressing ten or fifteen tons of these captured denizens of the deep. The rapidity with which this work is done until the fish in the boats are the fish in the great tubs for pickling is interesting. Each does his own part, and all work together like machinery. Meanwhile, if the day has been successful, at no expense of time, occasional jokes and laughs are heard among the many busy workers at the

Harbor, and the occasional inquiry,—"Who is high-hook to-day?"

When several parties have fished together in the same boat they divide the fish by a rule of their own invention, and with dispatch. If one owns a boat and has a partner in fishing they throw the fish ashore, and then divide them one by one into three piles, one pile earned by the boat for its owner. As soon as all are thus evenly divided one of the partners turns his face away from the three piles, while the other, unseen, points to one after another of the piles, saying,—"Whose is that?" and the answers from the other settle the division for the day, and each then dresses his own. Meanwhile livers are saved for oil to cure consumptives, boys are there getting the sounds, and farmers are busy with their carts and oxen getting the offal for their land. By five o'clock the work of the day is nearly over, the frequent click of the fish-house lock is heard, and little squads of weary fishermen are seen propelling their heavy feet homeward to be greeted by happy wives and children and to enjoy the well prepared meal, and the refreshing sleep for which they often retire earlier than does the "unwearied sun."

Occasionally the "voyge" is much more abruptly and less profitably ended, as when a sudden storm, in the early part of the day, comes down upon that little fleet like a hawk swooping down upon a brood of chickens. Then a speedy return to the Harbor begins, in some cases before a hook has been dropped, or an anchor cast. At such a time spy-glasses from many windows on the Island are pointing towards the fleet, as the storm has increased with great rapidity. Then anxious wives, and mothers, and children have gathered upon the shore and watched for returning kindred. Previous to the Government Harbor such occasions were exceedingly perilous, as the danger of landing in the high and violent surf was so great. The most graphic description would be only a feeble outline of the terrible reality. At such a time behold that darkening cloud coming on the swift wings of the wind, accompanied with the sudden roughness of the sea occasioned by the rapidly traveling storm from a distance, while the fisherman's homeward boat is in imminent peril. He hastens with all sail, but when he reaches the Bay the danger from breakers along the shore is equal to that on the deep. He hesitates to land, while death seems to be boarding his vessel. With his crew of two or three he sees his kindred on the shore in agony. Knowing well the fury of those mad breakers, by the most skillful exertions he skims over the waves this way and that in the Bay until remaining there seems to be fatal. Then, in that moment of desperation, when the only chance of reaching the shore alive is to ride the highest breaker, hear the captain say, as one now living has said,—"Boys, we shall be drowned if we stay here, and we may as well try to go ashore!" Now the little vessel is headed for the landing. Rapidly she glides to safety or destruction. Eyes upon the shore fill with tears, hands are wrung in agony, lips quiver as their whispered prayer is breathed like Peter's into the storm. She is seen to have selected the strong shoulders of the largest of the "three brothers,"—the wave that may carry her so high upon the shore that the next wave cannot reach and strike her, and thus afford the fishermen a moment in which to escape. "Steady! steady! Not too fast," says an old seaman on the shore. For if the boat gets too far upon said shoulders she will pitch over and be buried in an instant. Neither must she lag behind, for if she does the receding wave will swamp her instantly. Her sail is raised or lowered by the inch according to the command of the captain at the helm, to keep her balanced on that wave. "She rides! She rides!" says another in suppressed, anxious, hopeful tones, among others standing in breathless silence, while the critical instant of life or death hastens, and the great wave carries the little craft high upon the land, the fishermen are safe, and the "big brother" retires to the deep, like Jonah's whale.

We can easily imagine that boat to have only one codfish in it, but can hardly imagine a buyer beating the fisherman's price down from six to five cents a pound.

Summer fishing by the Islanders is carried on chiefly in Pounds, and with seine and hooks. The seine is used for catching blue fish and mackerel principally, and this branch increases with the increasing demands of the hotels and boarding-houses in the watering season, when so many enjoy the great luxury of the choicest fish direct from the ocean.

From the various modes of catching the fish, the entire value of the Block Island fisheries may safely be estimated at seventy-five thousand dollars annually. This estimate is made only in reference to the Island, while many vessels from abroad fish there for cod, mackerel, sword-fish, etc., and enjoy the benefits of the Harbor.

Whales in considerable numbers have hovered about the Island late years, and fishing for them has been contemplated, and if successfully undertaken prescriptions may be furnished according to the recommendation to a professional gentleman on his way to the Island who remarked that he had been told the fish there were good to invigorate the brain, and asked one of his traveling companions this question,—"How much fish would you advise me to eat to bring up my brain?" "About *one-half of a whale a day*," was the reply.

These monsters of the deep fear the fishermen about as much as the latter fear them. When close to a boat one, a few years ago, looked at the frightened father and son, and they looked at him, until, by sinking quietly down out of sight, he exemplified the saying,—"The fear of you, and the dread of you, shall be upon every beast of the earth, and upon every fowl of the air, upon all that moveth upon the earth, and upon *all the fishes of the sea.*" (Gen. ix, 2.)

SAILOR PHRASES.

These were formerly very common among the fishermen on the Island before the local dialect there was *corrupted* by the hosts of visitors from abroad. Some of them to a landsman are very forcible and by no means devoid of beauty. Paul could not find a better expression for his feelings than the sailor phrase which he used when he spoke of his "desire to depart," etc. They are amusing, sometimes, to a stranger.

Two grown brothers were crossing a field. Sam had high and tight boots, Edwin had not. As they came to a wet, soft place Sam took Edwin on his back to carry him over. While on their way they dramatized Bunyan's Slough of Despond. Sam was heavy, and Edwin was a heavy pack, and Sam began to sink. He exerted himself with all his might, and thus sprained his leg so that he could do nothing. This dismounted Edwin, and both wallowed in the mire, until Edwin got Sam on *terra firma.* Then Edwin, more alarmed, as he saw his brother unable to stand, than if he had been in a shipwreck, ran for the doctor, and exclaimed to him,—"I want you to go as quick as you can, for I was on Sam's back crossing a slough and he *carried away his leg!*"

The comparison of a man with a disabled leg to a dismasted ship for a while "carried away" the doctor with a hearty laugh.

In a similar sense an Islander who had lost off a button expressed his uneasiness by saying that his suspender was "carried away."

The following is a specimen prepared especially for the writer in the winter of 1874.

Directions for walking from the Harbor to the Neck School-House.

Heave along the beach till you make the first port light round the Sand Head.

Steer away for that light (in a window) till you make the Sand Head.

Then wear away to the nor'ad till you make the next port light. Then steer away for that till you make the stone wall.

Then bear away to the nor'ad, and keep her steady till you make the School-house light on the starboard.

Many a time in the dark evenings of winter the writer found these directions to be valuable while walking along the shore of the "loudly sounding sea" on his way to some of the best school-house meetings ever attended.

THE HARBORS OF BLOCK ISLAND.

"*There was no harbor.*" This first record on the subject was made in 1660, in the original agreement to purchase and settle the Island. Five years afterwards the settlers petitioned the Court of Rhode Island for help to build a harbor, and this petition was presented by Thomas Terry. The Governor, his Deputy, and Mr. John Clarke were appointed to look into the matter by visiting the Island. In 1670, as nothing seems to have been done, the same petition was repeated by Thomas Terry and Hugh Williams, and in response the Rhode Island Assembly appointed a committee of two, Caleb Carr, and Joseph Torrey of Newport, to raise contributions "to make a convenient harbor there, to the encouradging fishing designs." About ten years after this some visible results of this movement appeared.

The Great Pond Harbor was the first with which the Island was favored. This was constructed by a Harbor Company organized on the Island in 1680, assisted by a town tax. Capt. James Sands was the leading man in this Company, while Simon Ray was Chief Warden before whom, Sept. 14, 1686, others were acknowledged as new members. This enterprise was a failure, and the Harbor Company, in July, 1694, surrendered its charter. This, however, was followed with repeated but unsuccessful efforts on the part of the town, and of private individuals until June, 1705, when the whole enterprise was abandoned, the difficulty in managing the Breach was so great. The principal reason assigned for this abandonment was that by "the providence of God a prodigious storm hath broken down the above said harbor."

The New Harbor, or Pier, was in use in 1709, and the town had a graded tax on foreign vessels for entering this harbor. From this, in 1717, mention was made of the "Harbor Bay," and in this year a tax for fastening at the Pier was levied by the town, but was repealed in 1718. This Harbor was serviceable about twelve years, and then was destroyed by a storm.

The New Pier. After the former had been swept away, after state and town appropriations for a new harbor, after a joint committee had begun "cutting a passage through the beach," this project was stopped in February, 1735, by an act of the General Assembly, which at the same time appropriated £1,200 for "making an addition to the old Pier, or building a new one." The work of building a new one was retarded by frequent storms. The State appropriated £200 more, and in June, 1743, £400 more, making £1,800 in all. In May, 1845, the State Committee, consisting of Samuel Rodman, Teddeman Hull, and Abel Franklin, reported on the New Pier to the Assembly that they "found it to be completely finished." This costly structure could not endure the heavy seas that beat upon the Island.

The Lottery Harbor was projected in 1762. A charter for

a lottery to obtain means for another harbor was granted, but was not successful. This contemplated another trial of the Great Pond for a harbor. This project was renewed in 1773, contemplating an appropriation from town and state combined with a lottery. In the record then made it is said:—

"The place now proposed for opening a communication with the sea is about a quarter of a mile southward from the old channel, where the water is much deeper," etc. (Col. Rec., viii, 209.)

The Pole Harbor was begun about the year 1816, about fifty years after the Lottery Harbor efforts had been dispelled by the approaching Revolution. This was an individual enterprise, each man, as he chose, at low tide, setting his own spiles where they are now seen, near the Government Harbor. At one time these poles were over one thousand in number. They did good service to the generation now passing away, although quite inadequate to the wants of the public.

The Government Harbor. The first act of Congress in favor of this was in 1838, calling attention of the Departments to the subject, but nothing definite was accomplished. Nearly thirty years afterward the subject was again brought before Congress in an able speech by Senator Sprague of Rhode Island, and about the same time Hon. Nicholas Ball appeared before the Senate Committee, as a citizen of Block Island, of which the Boston *Journal* then said,—"The Committee were so impressed by Mr. Ball's plain facts they voted to recommend an appropriation of $40,000. This was followed by a thorough government survey of the Island for the best location of the harbor, and special attention was given to the Great Pond, and without knowing the old Island records of former experiments with the Great Pond, the surveyors came to conclusions of necessary failures corresponding with failures that had

78   HISTORY OF BLOCK ISLAND.

long since occurred and had passed from the knowledge of the public. After great effort on the part of many, and especially of Hon. Nicholas Ball, and of Hon. Senator H. B. Anthony of Rhode Island, in July, 1870, Congress made an appropriation of $30,000 for a Government Harbor at Block Island. Its construction was begun in October, 1870. In the March following Congress made another appropriation, of $75,000, and in June of 1872, it made a third, of $50,000, and under this appropriation Hon. J. G. Sheffield of Block Island completed his contract to place 10,000 tons of stones in the Breakwater. These sums, amounting to $155,000, paid for doing the work, the cost of which, in 1868, the United States Board of Engineers estimated at $372,000.

WRECKS.

For many years Block Island has been noted for the wrecks upon its shores. These have resulted from its location, and from fogs, and treacherous tides between it and Long Island. But few of these sad spectacles are here given, as specimens of many of a similar character.

One probably occurred in its vicinity in the year 1704, as at that time a body floated ashore and received special attention from the citizens. Captain Edward Ball was then "Crown Officer," or sheriff of the Island, and by right of his office he summoned a jury of inquest, who, after "solemn" examination, rendered this verdict,—"We find no wounds that occasioned his death, but we conclude that the water hath been his end, or cause of his death." This act at least indicates their humanity.

The Mars, in 1781, was driven upon the Island by one of our war vessels. She was an English merchantman, laden with goods which were sold by the sheriff of Kent County, Rhode Island.

The Ann Hope, about the year 1815, an East Indiaman,

owned by Brown & Ives of Providence, went ashore on the south end of the Island, in the vicinity of Black Rock, in a snow storm in the night, Captain Lang in command. When she was discovered in the morning by the Islanders the fearful scene beggared description. She was going to pieces, as her keel hung fast to the rocky shore. Her upper deck, on which were several cannon for fighting pirates who then infested the seas, had separated from the hull and was floating away upon the tide. Her cargo of spices, leather, and various kinds of merchandise was drifting here and there, while the Islanders were saving some of the articles that came ashore, among which were a few bags of coffee, until in a short time all were borne away by the tide. Meanwhile all possible efforts were made to save the perishing, some of whom were rescued, and the lifeless bodies of others, as they drifted ashore, were taken and buried decently by the inhabitants on the bluff overlooking the place of the sad disaster. Old men of the Island, in pitiful tones, have many a time recounted the heart-rending scenes of the lost "Ann Hope." One of them, however, Mr. Amad Dodge, who naturally had a keen sense of the ludicrous, generally closed his narrative with a good laugh, as he described one of the wrecked sailors who proved his enjoyment of the stimulant given him, and the manipulations of the Islanders to resuscitate him. He appeared so much like a corpse, and others were in so much need of assistance, that one of his manipulators said to the other,—"Let us try to save that one out there in the water, for this man is as good as dead!" Whereupon the latter, who was supposed to be in a hopeless condition, exclaimed, as if impatient for more stimulant,— "Na! indade, I'm as good as a half a dozen dead men!" He was an Irishman.

THE WARRIOR.

The *Warrior*, a large two-mast schooner, carrying goods and passengers between Boston and New York, was wrecked on Sandy Point in April, 1831. That Point, the extreme north end of the Island, then extended considerably farther out into the Sound than at present. The Warrior, becalmed in the previous evening at the eastward of the Island, had drifted until she was completely land-locked by the side of the Point, where she found herself early the next morning, while the wind was blowing a heavy gale, and the Sound was foaming with whitecaps. All human effort to change her course was unavailing. No life-saving apparatus was at hand. Stalwart Islanders hastened to the shore. The vessel, drifting rapidly, must soon be dashed to pieces. The following letter, from Mr. Benjamin T. Coe, then the Inspector of Customs for Block Island, and a witness of the wreck, was written to John C. Morrison, Esq., of New York:—

"*Dear Sir*,—Yours of the 19th has come to hand this day. There were no goods saved from the Warrior, of the description you mentioned.

" It is impossible to describe the awful situation of that vessel when she first came on shore, the sea breaking over her masts, and seven souls hanging to her rigging, not more than one hundred and fifty yards from us, and completely out of the power of man to render any assistance—the vessel striking so hard as to drive her bottom up, both masts unstepped, and fell, at the same time ripped up her main deck and the goods immediately washed out of her and drove away to the eastward. Some cotton and calico drove ashore here, one sack of hides, something like forty dozen carpenters' rules, etc. What goods were saved I delivered to Mr. Charles Brown, the Agent from Boston, and Mr. Charles M. Thurston of Newport, to whom I must refer you.

"I am informed there were thirty tons of iron in the bottom of the vessel, which is, I think, now buried up with sand, as there has been no part of said bottom seen about the Island. When the weather grows warmer I intend to make an examination for the bottom of the vessel. It may be the case that some heavy articles can be found. If anything of the kind you mention should be found I will give you the earliest information in my power. Our insulated situation renders it very difficult—we have no chance of writing, only when our boats go off, and that is not frequent.

"Your ob't servant,
BENJAMIN T. COE."

Other witnesses tell essentially the same story, with some additional particulars. One has described the sand-bar from the shore to the ship as sometimes nearly naked between the heavy seas passing over the Point. One of the crew, large and resolute, used great exertion to keep his imperiled companions from becoming chilled and benumbed by the cold wind, by his keeping them active. Finally, as he saw no hope of assistance from the hundreds on the shore, he made the desperate effort of running on the sand-bar to the land between two monstrous waves, but when half way to land he saw a violent, high sea coming upon him, and he bravely turned and met it head foremost. He might as well have met an Alpine avalanche. His dead body soon after was picked up on the beach. Others on the wreck lashed themselves to the deck, and after the storm were taken off by the Islanders, all dead and blackened by the bruises received from the débris violently thrown hither and thither by the angry waves. That was a solemn day when seven corpses from the Warrior were lying side by side upon the green bank not far from the wreck. Captain Scudder, all of his crew and passengers, finished life's voyage together in that worst of places in a gale, where two seas meet.

The Islanders made respectable coffins for the unfortunate strangers, laid them out decently, and had religious services at their burial. Their seven graves may now be seen in the northwest corner of the Cemetery on the Island. Captain Scudder and his mate, it is said, have been removed by their friends, who were happily surprised in finding their dead so kindly cared for by the hands of strangers.

The whole number of lives lost by the wreck of the Warrior, there is reason to believe, was twenty-one, fourteen of whom drifted away never to be seen again until the sea shall give up its dead. Mr. Anthony Littlefield, who witnessed the sad disaster, while in Boston soon after, heard a man say that he was on board the Warrior just before she sailed, and that she then had in all twenty-one —eighteen men, two women, and a colored maid-servant.

This fearful wreck is said to have been the result of carelessness on the part of the watch, who did not give timely warning of danger. Mr. Weeden Gorton, while watching the wreck, says he saw men jump overboard like sheep while the Warrior was going to pieces.

THE MOLUNCUS.

The Moluncus, a brig, stranded on Block Island, at Grace's Point, in 1855, an account of which is here given, in part, to indicate the mettle of the Island sailors in the midst of great dangers at sea. A very severe storm drove her ashore about evening. The Island Wrecking Company were soon at hand and bantering to get her off. As she was so fast aground her captain, crew, and the wreckers all left her, and on shore went to the house of Robert C. Dunn, a short distance from the vessel. There they bantered some time about the price of getting her off and into port. At last the agreement was made, the condition being

$2,500. Each party took a copy of the contract. By this time it was quite dark, rain falling, and the wind blowing a gale. But the wreckers decided to examine the vessel as far as possible to determine what *gear* to apply to her in the morning. But when they reached the place where they left her, behold *she was gone!* What was to be done? They were bound to get her into port by the stipulation. To lose her was to lose a fine sum of money. But how could she be found in such a night? The furious waves were coming towards them and madly breaking at their feet, waves accompanied by winds howling fearfully, while over all brooded thick darkness. That wind moved an Island barn from its foundations. They had neither light nor compass, and only a frail surf-boat with which to venture upon such a sea. Yet, without parley, the more daring seized their boat, shoved it into the teeth of the wind and waves, and one after another leaped in and pushed off, with Capt. N. L. Willis, Frank Willis, Sylvanus Willis (three brothers), Simon Ball, Wm. P. Ball, Silas Mott, S. R. Allen, Luther Dickens, and Thomas Rathbone, and launched to search for the lost brig in the storm and darkness. Soon they were out at sea, tossed here and there, at the mercy of wind, waves, tide, and darkness. The direction of the wind was their only guide. Anxious thoughts flit across their minds occasionally as they continued the search for the faintest outlines of the vessel, but none could be seen. At last, when hope deferred began to make the hearts of some sick, through the spray and darkness something like the shadow of a ship appeared. "Steady, boys! haul steady to wind'ard, for your lives!" said the Captain in an old "sea-dog" tone that meant what only sailors can fully understand. Soon all hearts grew light, and the oars were pulled with a force they had never felt from human hands before. Words were few. The brig was there, miles away from land, rocking in the deep troughs, with her tall masts swaying this way and that, almost lying flat, for an instant, upon the water. Her lee side was cautiously approached, and as its gunnel came to the water's edge, one leaped aboard, a line from her was made fast to the brave boat, and soon all were upon her broad deck, manning her sails, and heading for Newport, where their well-earned $2,500 in gold was promptly tendered by the Captain whose brig was got off by the rising tide, and by a most daring venture was found and sailed into port in good condition.

The only mishap among these wreckers was, they did not adhere strictly to their contract, and by bad advice, claimed salvage, spent about $1,000 at law, were defeated, and at last took the money stipulated for in the contract.

There have been times when so many wrecks occurred simultaneously on the Island that they almost suggest some general concert of action. The following are given as an instance.

THE MAYS.

These were two fine schooners wrecked on the Island in the spring of 1876. Their coincidences were remarkable. One was the *Catherine May*, Capt. Davis, the other was the *Henry J. May*, Capt. E. E. Blackman, from the same port, the same date; went ashore the same day, the 21st of May, at nearly the same point—the southwest part of the Island, one at 7:30 P. M.; the other thirty minutes after. The former was got off by the Old Wrecking Company, and taken to Newport for $2,000; and the latter by the same Company, and was taken to Fall River by two steamers for $3,000. These, with many others, would have been a total loss but for the prompt action of the wreckers.

WRECKING.

This does not mean, as some might think, the *producing* of wrecks, but the saving of vessels already stranded.

Although hard things have been said of the wreckers, and doubtless bad things have been done by them, yet they no more merit unqualified denunciation than do physicians who require large pay for great cures. Great dangers and expense are incurred in saving from total loss a vessel that has struck a sandy or a rocky shore.

William P. Lewis, Esq., of Block Island, Secretary of the Old Protection Wrecking Company there, has furnished the following facts of its business.

During the seventeen years previous to 1877 that company got off from the shores of the Island and Point Judith twenty-one schooners, five barks, and three brigs. The value of property thus saved was about one million and two hundred thousand dollars, besides the vessels saved by the New Company on the Island. During these seventeen years five schooners were wholly lost on the shores of the Island, valued at $120,000. The number of wrecks there from 1843 to 1860 are said to have been greater than those during the above named period. A great many steamers and sailing vessels have struck the Island, and by favorable wind and tide have got off without coming under the name of wrecks. But it may be safely said that millions have been lost by wrecks, and millions saved by wrecking on Block Island. These casualties are greatly diminished now by the government light-houses, fog signal, and life-saving stations, and signal stations there, and it is believed the time is not far distant when navigation shall be so well understood, and precautions so ample for the mariner, that these descriptions of former casualties will be read with interest. For this reason the following sketch of a wrecking process which the writer witnessed is here given.

The Laura E. Messer, a beautiful three-masted schooner, Captain J. F. Gregory, from Newport to Baltimore, in the winter of 1874-5, by some mysterious error, in a fair wind and not very dark night, ran upon Sandy Point. Her light cargo, a few hundred barrels of apples, and the delay of the Captain in securing the aid of the wreckers, afforded a fair opportunity to wind and tide to carry her high up on the sand bar, so that a high tide, strong wind, and a powerful *gear* were necessary to get her off, all of which made the work for the wreckers very perilous, as at that point the wind and rising tide produced a strong current on the east and west sides of the Island, and these currents met on that bar or point with such violence as had previously destroyed the *Warrior* in 1831, the fearful scene of whose perishing crew and passengers was still fresh in the minds of the wreckers, and the *L. E. Messer* was lying very near the identical spot where that sad catastrophe occurred.

To take this vessel off, imbedded as she was in the sand, required more power than any steamer could apply, and it must be incessant, and unyielding, against wind and tide, for perhaps weeks or months before the needed combination of power from wind, tide, and gear could take her from her bed.

The gear consisted of immense hawsers, smaller ropes, blocks, chains, heavy anchors, etc. An ingenious network of strong ropes over the deck fastened to stanchions, masts, and windlass distributed all the power to all her parts, and from these parts it was all concentrated upon two great hawsers that stretched from her bow to the wrecking anchors out in the deep water, one of them extending out twenty-one hundred feet. To this were attached three heavy anchors at proper distances from each other. The other hawser ran out parallel with the first nine hundred and sixty feet, and to this was added a heavy chain four hundred and fifty feet long, making this entire cable fourteen hundred and ten feet in length, and to this two large anchors were attached. Either of these five anchors was sufficient to hold a ship in an ordinary storm, but they all had a power applied to them simultaneously so great as to move them. This was done by the windlass and pulleys on the deck of the schooner—"The best windlass we've ever seen," said the old captains of the Island.

Trim and beautiful, with her tall three masts, there she sat in the sand, every timber in her groaning under the great strain from her anchors, while the harsh winds of winter night and day struck her sighing shrouds. Moons waxed and waned, tides rose and fell, storms from the wrong direction came and went, and only a little gain was secured by wheeling her bow off shore. Almanacs were consulted for moons and tides, and as the highest tides were at midnight, then the wreckers were ready for action. On the night of its highest point the wind blew a gale, and it was enough to make one grow pale to watch by moonlight the awful commotion of the angry elements a little farther out upon the Point than the place where the wreck was lying. There we had a perfect comment of Luke's meaning when he said—"two seas met." Not only was the sight appalling, but the sounds of the roaring winds and dashing waves were terrific. It was difficult for two standing face to face to understand each other's words.

At twelve in the night the wreckers were to be on deck. Some had spent the early part of the night aboard the wreck, while others slept in the Light-house, close by. At the appointed time it was very interesting to see the old "sea-lions" put on their sailor suits, light their pipes with the cool purpose of utilizing those fearful elements for mechanical purposes. They were temperate men, and said but little. They knew their danger. For if she should leave the beach, with them on her decks, and be hauled out to her anchors in that gale, her hawsers might chafe and break, and then she would be driven upon the Point where the *Warrior* was so suddenly torn to pieces while all on board perished. With the windlass a heavier strain was put upon the hawsers and anchors, her tall masts swayed a little, and our eyes were strained to see her "jump" from her bed of sand as the propitious tide and heavy sea should raise her up suddenly. But the wind changed, the tide fell, the waves were cut down, and she was left more deeply imbedded than ever.

How many more moons must wax and wane, and tides ebb and flow before another combination of favoring elements none could tell. How many pipes were filled and smoked after that, while discussing the damage likely to be done to that "$5,000 gear," none can guess. Weeks of watching and waiting the wreckers worried away. At last the day came. All hands were there in the night, and aboard. At sunrise the high tide and a heavy swell lifted her up, and the strain from her anchors and hawsers made her dart in an instant from the beach into the deep water. The "off shore" wind carried her beyond her five anchors, which wheeled her about, as if to take a farewell look of her place of confinement. The waves were high, and she rode them with seeming impatience; as if writhing to escape. Soon her last anchor was weighed, and her cables shipped, and like a thing of life spread her wings, headed for Newport, and seemed joyfully to say,—"Farewell to Sandy Point, and its Light-house"—

> "Set at the mouth of the Sound to hold
> The coast light up on its turret old,
> Yellow with moss and sea-fog mold."

LEGENDS.

Few, if any, people are without mysterious legends adorned with the fantasies of superstition. While witchcraft was scourging Europe, and making no little disturbance at Salem and Boston, it is not strange that some queer freaks of the imagination were experienced by the early

Pilgrims and their descendants on Block Island. Although the "horseshoe" has been less popular on the Island than it has been in London and Boston, yet its oldest inhabitants even now echo the suppressed words of weird legends told a century ago. In reference to these the writer once consulted an aged blind man of strong intellect and emotional powers who was familiar with the ancient Island legends. His relation of a few was a severe tax upon the nerves of his stoical hearer, who never again conferred with him on the subject. Indeed it is a blessing to the coming generations to be ignorant of the multitude of fictitious stories that once were related with truthful solemnity by old men and women to children trembling with fear in the chimney corner. It may be well to preserve a few as fossils of extinct creatures of distorted imaginations.

THE DANCING MORTAR.

This, though somewhat intermixed with another legend, has its own individuality. Like every ignis fatuus it has its foundation in a reality. The real seems to be this,— that when the ship *Palatine* stopped at Block Island and left her diseased and dying inmates, she either then or on her return from the West Indies left on the Island logs or blocks of lignum-vitae, from which the Islanders, then destitute of mills, made mortars for crushing their corn. Two of those mortars are now in existence, the one here described having been deposited by the writer in Rhode Island Hall of Brown University.

To test the authenticity of this legend of the Dancing Mortar, several of the oldest and most trustworthy Islanders were consulted concerning it separately, without informing one of the statements of the other. This was in the year 1876. Mrs. Margaret Dodge, eighty-six years old, of remarkably clear memory; Mr. Anthony Littlefield, and his wife, each eighty-four years old; Mr. and Mrs. John

Ball, both over seventy; Mrs. Caroline Willis, eighty-one; and others, all agreed that this mortar was from the ship *Palatine*. It was well known to have been kept and owned at the house once owned and occupied by the venerable Simon Ray, where several of the unfortunate passengers of the Palatine were hospitably received, and near which house are their graves. There it remained long after the Ray family had passed away, and his house was occupied by another family.

For a considerable period after this change the old Ray house was said to be haunted. But few, perhaps, of the present readers know how much this means, unless they are familiar with the old stories of chimney ghosts and such "hobgoblins" as Bunyan had in mind when he wrote the Pilgrim's Progress. In and around that house such sights and sounds were said to have been seen and heard as ordinary nerves protest against repeating in an attempted description. In comparison with them the modern fabrications of spiritualism, and the tricks of ventriloquists are puerile.

The Dancing Mortar, as a part of the furniture of that house so powerfully haunted, naturally shared in the mysterious endowments of its surroundings. Before contemplating some of its strange freaks, a view should be had of it in its present condition.

It is of lignum-vitae, fourteen inches high, about ten inches in diameter, and is nearly as heavy as would be the same bulk of stone, it is so hard. It would hold about four quarts. The grains of its fiber are diagonal, for the most part, and so interwoven as to prevent it from cracking by hard usage or from age. For a considerable time it was used as a splitting-block, and now bears the marks of the axe on its weather-worn, gray, and shabby exterior, made so by a half century's exposure to the storms of summer and winter. Its interior, which used to receive the corn and the pestle, now looks "aged and gray," and it is hoped the rosette of moss which it wore when placed in its modern and more classic home will long remain as an ornament of one of the relics of antiquity.

In its younger days it did its dancing, according to the legend, when the old house where it was had the reputation of being mightily haunted. Then, they say, while the inmates were conversing on common topics, or musing over the hauntings of the house, this mortar would begin to move, untouched by human hand, until it threw itself from its standing position upon its side, striking with a *thud* upon the floor. This in itself was sufficient to alarm the spectators. But this was only the first preparation for dancing. Its next move was to roll from one side of the room to the other, by some invisible impulse. At this the amazement of the inmates can better be imagined than described. We can picture to ourselves the lively times in that room, lighted by a wood fire in the evening, as men, women, and children dodged here and there to escape the touch of that haunted, rolling mortar, lest they too should be infected with its witchery. After this rolling came its final antics for the occasion. These, after a little respite, consisted of righting itself up again on end. Then came the *dancing*, as without visible springs, or the touch of visible hands, it bounded from the floor to the joists and floor overhead, and thus went up and down between the floors, varying its position from one part of the room to another. Admitting this to be so, what could have been more natural than for those inmates, at the beginning of that lonely, mysterious mortar waltz, to have danced a "quickstep" hurriedly out of the doors and windows!

One of the half dozen aged witnesses concerning this legend incidentally suggested, though unintended, a key to its solution. "La! yes," said she, "I've hear'n tell about that mortar when I was a child; it was at the house of

Mr. T. D———, *the old opium eater.*" There, in his brain, probably, the house haunting, and the mortar dancing legend originated.

This mortar has been well known for over a century. More than fifty years ago its old home, the Simon Ray house, was taken down, and a part of it was put into the new house, about one hundred yards distant, then built and now owned by the aged and highly esteemed Raymond Dickens, who from his youth has been intimately acquainted with this mortar. He knew it when used for a splitting-block. But for some reason, perhaps on account of its waywardness in former days, it was refused a place in the new dwelling, and, as if to keep it quiet ever after, it was placed in a fence wall, on its side, with heavy stones on it, and there, for nearly fifty years, it did penance until liberated by the writer in 1876, and was honored with its present home,—

"Where Fame's proud temple shines afar."

Perhaps some legend seeker, at some future day, will learn the weird stories associated with the long and lonely path on the Island anciently known as "*the devil's causeway.*" See Refugees, for "Harbor Boys" legend.

THE PALATINE.

The legend of the ship *Palatine* is the most noted of any one that ever originated on Block Island. None other, perhaps, in our country has a more perfect commingling of fact and fiction, prose and poetry, pathos and tragedy, truth and falsehood, than this phantom ship story as understood by many.

That there was once a ship by the name of Palatine is quite certain. This is the nucleus of all the fictitious pyrotechnics concerning her transmutation into a mysteriously manned ship of fire, making brief voyages on Block

Island Sound for the benefit of poets and lovers of the marvelous.

An effort has been made, on the ground of mere assumption, to show that this vessel originally had some other name, but what it was we are not told. This assumption is that she received, at Block Island or elsewhere, the name Palatine from her Palatinates, or passengers of that name. But as well might we call a ship *Ireland* because she happens to be laden with Irish emigrants. Were sailors, as were the Islanders, ever known to call a vessel by any other name than that borne upon her hull? No. *Palatine* was her original name, whatever the nationality of her passengers.

This is demonstrated by a few authentic facts. Mr. Raymond Dickens, now about eighty years old, a native of the Island, hale, and of good memory, said to the writer that when he (Dickens) was a boy he frequently heard his grandfather, Thomas Dickens, at the age of about eighty, speak of the *ship Palatine*, not of the "Palatinates." By the memories of these two Islanders our minds are carried back to about 1736, and Simon Ray, one of the first proprietors of the Island, was then living. At his or at his son's house the invalid passengers of the Palatine were kindly received. He talked with Thomas Dickens about the Palatine; Thomas talked about her with his grandson Raymond Dickens, who is now living, and the nearest of these few links in the unbroken chain of evidence that a ship with her original name *Palatine* once came to Block Island.

A part of her legend is that she was somehow changed into a ship of fire, rising up from the waters of Block Island Sound, which separates the Island from the main land, and gracefully sailing on this tack or that, mysteriously manned by an invisible captain and crew, until hull, spars, ropes, and sails all slowly vanished in the air or settled down into the deep. Nor was all of this a myth, or an *ignis-fatuus*. For there is ample evidence that a very strange light once performed very strange freaks over those waters. Such testimony as the following is too reliable to be discarded. It was most frequently and vividly apparent about the beginning of the present century. It attracted the attention of such men as Dr. Samuel Mitchell of New York City, who desired to find some one to explain the phenomenon, and Dr. Aaron C. Willey, an able physician, and then a resident of the Island, wrote as follows to Dr. Mitchell:—

"BLOCK ISLAND, Dec. 10, 1811.

"*Dear Sir*,—In a former letter I promised to give you an account of the singular light which is sometimes seen from this place. I now hasten to fulfill my agreement. I should long since have communicated the fact to the literary world, but was unwilling to depend wholly upon the information of others, when by a little delay there was a probability of my receiving ocular demonstration. I have not, however, been fortunate in this respect, as I could wish, having had only two opportunities of witnessing this phenomenon. My residing nearly six miles from the shore which lies next to the region of its exhibition, and behind elevated ground, has prevented me from seeing it so frequently, perhaps, as I might otherwise have done. The people who have always lived here are so familiarized to the sight that they never think of giving notice to those who do not happen to be present, or even of mentioning it afterwards, unless they hear some particular inquiries made.

"This curious irradiative rises from the ocean near the northern point of the Island. Its appearance is nothing different from a blaze of fire. Whether it actually touches the water, or merely hovers over it, is uncertain, for I am informed that no person has been near enough to decide accurately. It beams with various magnitudes, and appears to bear no more analogy to the *ignis fatuus* than it does to the aurora borealis. Sometimes it is small, resembling the light through a distant window, at others expanding to the highness of a ship with all her canvas spread. When large it displays a pyramidal form, or three constant streams. In the latter case the streams are somewhat blended together at the bottom, but separate and distinct at the top, while the middle one rises higher than the other two. It may have the same appearance when small, but owing to distance and surrounding vapors cannot be clearly perceived. The light often seems to be in a constant state of insulation, descending by degrees until it becomes invisible, or resembles a lurid point, then shining anew, sometimes with a sudden blaze, at others by a gradual increasement to its former size. Often the instability regards the luster only, becoming less and less bright until it disappears, or nothing but a pale outline can be discerned of its full size, then returning to its former splendor in the manner before related. The duration of its greatest and least state of illumination is not commonly more than two or three minutes. This inconstancy, however, does not appear in every instance.

After the radiance seems to be totally extinct it does not always return in the same place, but is not unfrequently seen shining at some considerable distance from where it disappeared. In this transfer of locality it seems to have no certain line of direction. When most expanded this blaze is generally wavering like the flame of a torch; at one time it appears stationary, at another progressive. It is seen at all seasons of the year, and for the most part in the calm weather which precedes an easterly or a southerly storm. It has, however, been noticed during a severe northwestern gale, and when no storm immediately followed. Its continuance is sometimes transient, at others throughout the night, and it has been known to appear several nights in succession.

"This blaze actually emits luminous rays. A gentleman whose house is situated near the sea informs me that he has known it to illuminate considerably the walls of his room through the windows. This happens only when the light is within a half a mile of the shore, for it is often seen blazing at six or seven miles distant, and strangers suppose it to be a vessel on fire."

Dr. Willey, who then had and still has respectable relatives on the Island, and who well knew the superstitious notions of many in those days, both upon the Island and upon the shore opposite, in the same letter states that when he saw the Palatine light in the evenings of February, 1810, and December 20th of that year, its appearances were essentially the same as those above mentioned.

In reference to the now famous legend he, seventy years ago, said,—"From this time, it is said, the Palatine light appeared, and there are many who firmly believe it to be a ship of fire, to which their fantastic and distempered imaginations figure masts, ropes, and flowing sails." He finally adds,—

"I have stated facts to you, but feel a reluctance to hazard any speculations. These I leave to you and other acute researchers of created things. Your opinion I would be much pleased with.

"With the highest feelings of respect,

  (Signed) AARON C. WILLEY.
Hon. S. L. Mitchell."

From the above candid statement of facts by so respectable an eye-witness, and from ample corroborative testimony from others, there is left no ground of reasonable doubt that a phenomenal light, during the earliest part of the nineteenth century, was frequently seen gliding to and fro like a fairy yacht of ghostly pleasure seekers, enlarging and diminishing, changing from one style of craft to another, sinking and rising and tacking without helm or yards as if self-directed. Of its frequent spectators Whittier has the following beautiful stanzas,—

> "Nor looks nor tones a doubt betray,
> 'It is known to us all,' they quietly say;
> 'We too have seen it in our day.'
>
> "For still on many a moonless night,
> From Kingston Head and from Montauk Light,
> The specter kindles and burns in sight.
>
> "Now low and dim, now clear and higher,
> Leaps up the terrible Ghost of fire;
> Then slowly sinking the flames expire.
>
> "And the wise Sound skippers, though skies be fine,
> Reef their sails when they see the sign
> Of the blazing wreck of the Palatine."

In this Palatine legend, then, we have these well-authenticated facts: *first*, that there was a ship Palatine once in the waters of Block Island; and *second*, that in Block Island Sound there appeared a strange fire or light fed by an invisible fuel, frequently assuming the form of a three-masted vessel, moving about. Of this phenomenon no satisfactory explanation has ever been given, while much talent has been employed in making it instrumental in gratifying the taste for the marvelous. It is possible, however, that this light was fed by gas rising through the water, as the same invisible fuel has been known to rise hundreds of feet through the ground, and on the surface ignite and send up a flame forty feet high, and support this flame night and day for weeks, during a period of a score of years. This statement can be verified by respectable citizens in the vicinity of Canandaigua, N. Y., where burning springs were no novelty fifty years ago. The writer has seen the stream, once known as the "Burning Brook," in a certain neighborhood, where the flames used to play over its rapid surface, as the stream was gliding over a rock from whose fissures he saw bubbles of gas rising through the water. He there conversed with those who had applied the match near the surface of the water of this brook, and as a result they had seen flames rise and dance over the limpid stream as fantastically as did those

"Of the blazing wreck of the Palatine."

The gas on the Sound may have been ignited by electricity, as houses and barns are sometimes ignited by lightning.

It would be gratifying, were it possible, to give as definite a description of the ship Palatine, as we have of the Palatine Light. But during several years of research among the records of the Island the writer has never found a word that refers to this vessel. By request, Mr. Charles E. Perry, a native of the Island, and a gentleman whose scholarship and extensive research concerning the Palatine entitle him to a high degree of confidence, has prepared the following:—

"*Memoranda of Facts and Traditions connected with the Palatine.*

"She came ashore on Sandy Point, the northern extremity of Block Island, striking on the *Hummuck*, at that time a little peninsula of the Island. As the tide rose she floated off, and was towed into Cow Cove, near the Point, by the Islanders in their boats. The passengers were all landed, except one woman who refused to leave the wreck, and most of them were carried to the houses of Edward Sands (where John Revoe Paine, Esq., now lives), and Simon Ray, who owned a large part of the West Side, and lived in a house near the one now occupied and owned by Mr. Raymond Dickens. Many of the passengers, weakened by starvation and disease, soon died, and were buried on a little elevation west of the house of Wm. P. Lewis, Esq., where their graves are now visited.

"Some of the passengers, however, lived and left the Island, and one of them gave to the little daughter of Edward Sands, then twelve years old, a dress of India calico or chintz patches, as the material was then called. This little girl was my grandmother's grandmother, and my grandmother has often heard her relate this incident. My grandmother's grandmother died in 1836, at the age of ninety-six, from which data (she being twelve years old when the ship came ashore) I conclude that she was wrecked about the year 1752.

"One of these passengers, a woman, married a colored slave belonging to a Mr. Littlefield. Her name was Kate, and was commonly called *Kattern*. She was known as Long Kate to distinguish her from another who was then called Short Kate. The former had three children, *Cradle*, whose descendants have died or moved away; *Mary*, from whose descendants "Jack," a colored man, long in the employment of Hon. Nicholas Ball, and remembered by many as the driver of the four-ox team that took the visitors, in former days, from the Ocean View to the Bathing Beach; and *Jenny*, whose posterity have died and left the Island."

From Mr. Perry's replies to his extensive inquiries concerning the Palatine he has furnished the following extracts:—

"*Charles Mueller, U. S. Consul at Amsterdam*, July 4, 1870, states that the Custom House Archives there have been searched," and that "the record was found of a ship *Palatine* which was wrecked in the Bay of Bengal, July 14, 1784."

"*Richard H. Dana, Jr.*, states that his father's poem—THE BUCCANEER, was simply a work of imagination, founded on no fact, and having no reference to the Palatine."

J. G. Whittier states that his first hint of the story of its wreck came from James Hazard of Newport, that his knowledge on the subject is very limited, and that he has a plate said to have come from the Palatine."

From the foregoing facts Mr. Perry, as an intelligent Islander, gives us the following conclusions, from which others, of course, are at liberty to dissent if they see reasons for so doing. He says:—

"The gist of the traditional accounts of her seems to be, that she sailed from some German port, laden with well-to-do emigrants, bound to Philadelphia; that the captan died or was killed on the passage; that the officers and crew starved and plundered the helpless emigrants, and finally, in their boats, abandoned the vessel, which drifted ashore, as previously stated, during the week between Christmas and New Year's." *

"The ship was undoubtedly burned.

CHARLES E. PERRY."

Mr. Benjamin Sprague's Recollections about the Palatine.

He, a native Islander, when eighty-eight years old, with no disease preying upon his constitution, and with a clear memory, says he heard his parents say much about *Kattern*, one of the passengers from the Palatine. They called her "Dutch Kattern," which indicates her origin, and it was well understood by them that she came from the Palatine. Mr. Sprague, many years ago, well knew Kattern's daughter, Cradle, a mulatto, as Kattern married a negro soon

---

* This reference to Christmas suggests that tradition got the Palatine mixed up with the Golden Grove, a brig from Halifax that was wrecked, about a century ago, near Sandy Point, on Grove Point, which derives its name from that brig which came ashore on Christmas, and the crew who remained upon the Island commemorated the event by the poetry still repeated on the Island, in which are the lines,—

"From Halifax, that frozen shore,
On Christmas day we made the shore
On Block Island," etc.

after she came upon the Island. From Mr. Sprague we obtain a clue to the origin of the legend of the Palatine. He says she reported that the crew starved the passengers to get their money; that she was a noted fortune-teller; that she would hide away behind a wall, or in a thicket of bushes, and there lie in a trance for hours. On returning to the house much exhausted, and being asked where she had been, her reply was that she had been home to Holland, and then would give an account of her kindred there as she had just seen them. She lived on the Neck, and was believed to be a witch. The Islanders were afraid of her. Mr. Sprague has no recollection of ever having heard any account of the *burning* of the Palatine. Whether this part of the legend originated on the Island or on the main land we are unable to ascertain. Mr. Whittier, in answer to inquiry on the subject, said:—

"21st, 10 mo., 1876.

"*Dear Friend:*—

"In regard to the poem *Palatine*, I can only say that I did not intend to misrepresent the facts of history. I wrote it after receiving a letter from Mr. Hazard of Rhode Island, from which I certainly inferred that the ship was pillaged by the Islanders. He mentioned that one of the crew to save himself clung to the boat of the wreckers, who cut his hand off with a sword. It is very possible that my correspondent followed the current tradition on the main land.

"Mr. Hazard is a gentleman of character and veracity, and I have no doubt he gave the version of the story as he had heard it.

"Very Truly Thy Friend,
JOHN G. WHITTIER."

His poetic version of the wreck is mainly this:—

> "The ship that a hundred years before,
> Freighted deep with its goodly store,
> In the gales of the equinox went ashore.
>
> "The eager Islanders one by one
> Counted the shots of her signal gun,
> And heard the crash as she drove right on.
>
> "Into the teeth of death she sped;
> (May God forgive the hands that fed
> The false lights over the Rocky Head!)
>
> "O men and brothers! What sights were there!
> White upturned faces, hands stretched in prayer!
> Where waves had pity, could ye not spare?
>
> "Down swooped the wreckers like birds of prey,
> Tearing the heart of the ship away,
> And the dead had never a word to say.
>
> "And there with a ghastly shimmer and shine,
> Over the rocks and the seething brine,
> They burned the wreck of the Palatine.
>
> "In their cruel hearts as they homeward sped,
> 'The sea and the rocks are dumb,' they said,
> 'There'll be no reckoning with the dead.'"

Much of the report of the Palatine barbarity is traceable to one *Mark Dodge*, an Islander, and a maniac, who, it is said by good authority, burned the only windmill then upon the Island. He is said to have been silent when the Palatine was named to him, and from this silence it has been insinuated that he participated in her wreck and burning. But this is hardly sufficient testimony to make an intelligent person believe that a Christian colony had been converted into a band of pirates.

There was a time, about one hundred and fifty years ago, when much was said of Block Island in connection with pirates, and yet the Islanders may have been entirely innocent of piracy. For an account of the capture of pirates

THE PALATINE.

from Block Island, and recovery of their money, in the case of the British pirates, see Colonial Hist. of N. Y., vol. iv, p. 512. Also, for an account of the pirate vessels Ranger and Fortune, headed for Block Island when captured by the Greyhound, in 1723, twenty-six of whose pirates were hung at Newport, on Gravelly Point, July 19, 1723, see R. I. Colonial Records, vol. iv, pp. 329 and 331.

In 1740 the Rhode Island General Assembly voted an appropriation of £13 13s. "for victuals and drink to the pirates at Block Island, and their guards." Many persons abroad may have heard frequent mention of "Block Island pirates," without distinguishing those desperate prisoners from the native citizens of the Island with whom the government could safely trust those criminals, which could not have been done if the Islanders had been piratical.

There is ample evidence of the civil and religious good order of Block Island from the time it was settled to the present. It bears a favorable comparison with any other part of New England. Its humanity to the shipwrecked is well authenticated. According to Mr. Perry's investigations the unfortunate passengers of the Palatine were kindly received by the Islanders, and from his research we can learn of only one ship Palatine from authentic records, and she was wrecked (not burned at Block Island) in the Bay of Bengal. In 1704, on finding a dead body floating near the shore the Islanders at once summoned a jury of inquest, and in 1755 the sloop *Martha and Hannah*, Capt. William Griffin, from Halifax to New York, was stranded on the Island. The captain was drowned, and the crew were brought ashore, and when his body was recovered, an inquest was held by town authority, and all was done that the best society could require. The very gravestones of the old Cemetery of the Island, as well as its written records of more than two centuries; and the relations of several of its families to Benjamin Franklin, to Maj.-Gen.

Nathaniel Greene, to Governors Ward and Greene of Revolutionary fame, to the Rev. Samuel Niles, a native of the Island, and the first student at college from Rhode Island; and also to Roger Williams, are an overwhelming protest against the defenceless calumny that the Islanders killed the inmates of the Palatine, and then burned the vessel. Why should they *burn* her? The writer has never been able to obtain an answer to this inquiry, and he does not believe any can be given that would bear a minute's investigation. If the author of our lying legend had said that the Islanders took the Palatine all to pieces, and carefully preserved every sail, every rope, every foot of her timbers, and every bolt, all of which were of great value to them, he would have had corroborative testimony in the nature of things. But everything is against the barbarous notion that,—

> "Over the rocks and the seething brine,
> They burned the wreck of the Palatine."

Even if she were burned, her burning would have no more connection with the strange light on the Sound than it would have with the moon. No one ever saw the name *Palatine* on that "Ghost of Fire," and there is no more reason for calling it by that name than there is for applying to it any other name.

This, then, seems to be a fair analysis of the legend of the Palatine: *that* it consists of two parts—*Facts*, and *Fiction*.

In the *first* part it is evident *that* there was a ship Palatine; *that* she landed diseased passengers on Block Island; *that* she was from Holland; *that* she was finally wrecked in the Bay of Bengal in 1784; *that* a strange light, called the Palatine Light, appeared upon what is now known as Block Island Sound, at the beginning of the nineteenth century; *that* this light at times had the appearance of a vessel; *that* it attracted much attention, but received no satisfactory explanation; and *that* it had no relation whatever to the ship Palatine.

In the *second*, or fictitious part of this legend we find much that seems traceable *to "Dutch Kattern,"* the low-bred woman who married a negro slave, was a fortune-teller, was believed to be a witch, and was a Palatine passenger; *to Mark Dodge*, the Island maniac and mill-burner, who was silent when he heard others talking of the Palatine; *to the Mr. Hazard* who gave his version to Mr. Whittier, and to others, in whose fancy the ship Palatine has had a transmigration into the mysterious light on the Sound.

The following version of the Palatine Legend from its venerable and well-known author will be read with interest for several reasons, and not least for the poetic genius which he has displayed. His impressions of the legend were formed in early life, when his father and brother lived in sight of Block Island, on the main land, and said brother was a teacher on the Island in the period of the appearance of the Palatine Light, and they were familiar with its existence on the Sound. Another witness of this Phenomenon who lived in Rhode Island just opposite to Block Island, wrote from Napoli, Cattaraugus Co., N. Y., March 4, 1878, as follows:—"About the burning Palatine ship."— "I have seen her eight or ten times or more. In those early days nobody doubted her being sent by an Almighty Power to punish those wicked men who murdered her passengers and crew. After the last of these were dead she was never more seen. We lived when I was young in Charlestown, directly opposite Block Island, where we used to have a plain view of the burning ship."—*"Benjamin Congdon."*

How she punished the guilty, and whether she punished them more than she did the innocent, are open questions.

THE PHANTOM SHIP.

(By Rev. A. G. Palmer, D.D., of Stonington, Conn.)

Abreast Point Judith's sea-girt light,
Whose radiance, intermittent, bright,
Cutting the thick and heavy night—

Lights up the rough Atlantic's wave,
The imperiled mariner to save,
From reef, and wreck, and yawning grave.

Some twenty miles away, or more,
The mirage, on Block Island's shore,
Herald's the "line gale" evermore.

This island, with its base of rock,
Formed in some geologic shock,
Seems a vast monolithic block,

Boldly, uprising from the sea,
As if from all eternity,
It had been anchored, there to be.

A huge breakwater, east and west,
Forming a lee, where ships might rest,
When by the fierce southeaster pressed,

Breaking the heavy swell and tide,
Against its clay-bound bluffs outside,
Despite the ocean's wrath and pride.

Southwest, some three leagues, bold Montauk,
Like Dover with its cliffs of chalk,
Rises, the spiteful tides to balk;

Sending abroad its glinting light
In alternating flashes bright,
Now seen, now unseen, through the night.

Northwest, six leagues, Stonington's ray
Blends with Watch Hill, across the Bay;
Point Judith, east, ten leagues away.

Across this land-locked intervale
Of ocean, white capped by the gale,
Vessels may scud, 'neath tight reefed sail

In summer, under genial skies,
The waves in languid wooings rise,
To kiss the earth that seaward lies.

With opening spring the hills are green,
And sheltered valleys warm between,
Stand early dressed in verdant sheen.

Its atmosphere, soothed and beguiled,
Of winter's chill, is pure and mild—
A bracing tonic undefiled.

Its granite soil, though not in wealth
Abounding, yet brings robust health—
A treasure free from "rust and stealth."

Its boats, two masted, sweep the sea
Around, with patient industry,
To find where choicest fish may be.

Often they drift across the main,
Bearing their piscatory gain,
To supplement their living plain.

At Stonington, in days gone by,
They came, at times, their trade to ply;
In their small way to sell and buy—

Changing the products of the sea,
For what their household's wants might be,
Tobacco, sugar, coffee, tea—

Returning with their little store,
With wife and children home once more,
Recounting their adventures o'er.

A rural hermit-like seclusion,
Free from the outside world's intrusion,
Good livelihood, but no profusion.

Here men and women lived and died,
Strangers alike to wealth and pride,
With their poor way well satisfied.

Religion here was honored too—
A faith unfeigned, primitive, true—
Pervading, now, the island through.

 * * * * * *

Let this suffice: I haste to tell,
A story, told by one so well
In part, no verse may his excel.

If but allowed to supplement
The Palatine, of Whittier's Tent
Upon the Beach, no compliment,

It matters not, from where or whence,
Or with what generous pretence,
Could be more grateful to my sense,

I tell the story as t'was told
In my young ears times manifold,
By gray haired men and very old,

And women too, as well as men,
With their loquacious acumen,
Described the how and where and when.

"Why, yes," they said, with knowing mien,
And nods significant between,
"The Phantom Ship we've often seen."

"Before a storm at edge of night,
Betwixt the darkness and the light,
The Palatine looms up to sight.

"Out of an overhanging cloud,
Unfolding from a misty shroud,
She sweeps, a ship, full rigged and proud,

"With sails all set, masts towering high,
Piercing the low, storm laden sky,
She seems about to pass us by.

"Then, as by some dire fate ruled o'er,
Despite the breakers' warning roar,
She tacks and plunges to the shore.

"And as she cuts through mist and haze,
A shimmering light runs up her stays,
The Phantom ship is all ablaze;

"Her yards and topmasts all alight,
Reddening the deepening gloom of night,
Fall to her deck, all glowing bright.

"Then with a fiery, hissing sound,
Amid the surging waters round,
She sinks into the depths profound."

Such is the story, which a child,
Many an evening's hour beguiled
With its recital weird and wild.

It may not in all parts agree,
With other versions, but will be
Simply as it was told to me.

I think I may, quite safely too,
Poetic license kept in view,
Assume the tale historic true.

* * * * * *

About one hundred years ago,
The time exact I do not know,
Occurred this frightful scene of woe,

A tragedy of black design,
And crime blood-red in every line:
The burning of the Palatine.

'Twas on an equinoctial night,
When sea-fowl, with instinctive fright,
Landward, for shelter, take their flight,

Dark clouds draped heavily the sky;
Shrouding the stars, God's lamps on high,
Hung out to cheer the sailor's eye.

While round the island's jagged shore,
The cold waves beat with muffled roar,
Their dirge of storms and shipwrecks o'er—

The wreckers, on the alert for game,
Hastened to send on high a flame,
The notice of some craft to claim.

Inland, on a commanding height,
They lit their beacon fire that night,
As if it were a headland light,

Placed there by Government, to say,
"No perils lie in your pathway,
The dangerous shore is far away."

Just then a ship from out the sky,
Sweeping, they watch with straining eye—
She would have passed the island by—

Had not that light lured her to keep
Her onward course, with unchecked sweep,
Pledging the waters, reefless, deep—

Onward she dashed, till struck the rock:
Shivering beneath the stunning shock,
She foundered in the fatal lock—

And then, the booming signal gun
Out on the air its message flung,
Telling the horrid crime was done.

The wreckers, at the lurid flash,
As if possessed of Demons rash,
Plunged to the shore with headlong dash:

Swift to their boats and oars they flew,
Cutting the crested billows through—
This outlaw, bandit, wrecking crew.

They pushed their keels, with oars astrain,
And with strong sinews, swept the main,
In hungry haste to clutch the gain—

And as they near the stranded wreck,
Their speed, with oars reversed, they check,
Sweep up her sides and pour on deck.

The crew and passengers, without
Misgivings or suspicious doubt,
Receive them with a cheer and shout,

But, as the flickering lights reveal
Dark brutal faces, o'er them steal
Grave apprehensions, for their weal.

The pirates now with manner rough,
And oaths, their courtesies rebuff,
And rifle them of all their stuff—

Wardrobe and every precious thing,
Necklace of gold and diamond ring
Into their bags, in haste, they fling.

The ship's rich freight and merchandise,
Her stores and plentiful supplies,
Of wealth a mingled sacrifice,

They smuggle hastily ashore,
Amid the breakers' dash and roar,
Till the last load is ferried o'er.

And then, 'mid shrieks, despairing wild,
From husband, wife, parent, and child,
Young man and maiden undefiled,

While knees were bent, in anguished prayer,
And women with disheveled hair,
Wailed fiercely out their blank despair,

They fired the ship; the flames shot high,
Flaring against the frowning sky,
Tinged to an angry fiery dye—

Tarred rope and sail and yard and spar
Threw up their ghastly streams afar,
The whole ship one huge blazing star.

And as the rigging burned and fell
Upon the deck, all helped to swell
The flaming of this floating hell.

No lives were spared; none left to swear
What deeds of horror were done there,
Under that night of black despair.

She burned down to the water's edge,
Then as if riven by a wedge,
Bilged on the underlying ledge.

So perished in that fearful night,
Not by neglect or oversight,
But by the wreckers' treacherous light,

By foul and murderous design,
And crime blood red in every line,
That goodly ship the Palatine.

* * * * * *

The next year as the autumn neared,
Leading the equinox, appeared
The staunch old ship, full rigged and steered

Boldly on to the fatal shore,
Where she had struck, the year before,
And sank, 'twas thought, to rise no more.

And, yearly, while one mutineer
Survived, did that old ship appear,
As the autumnal storm drew near,

Coming at dark amid the haze,
Of thickening tempest, all ablaze,
To meet the wrecker's guilty gaze;

Throwing, afar, her ghastly light,
As on that unforgotten night,
Then sinking, hissing out of sight.

But when the last old wrecker died,
The tempest howled and dashed the tide
Ashore with rage intensified.

The island with its wrath was shook,
In every corner every nook;
All faces wore a pallid look—

The thunder bellowed, lightnings flashed,
And billows in their fury lashed
The shore, and o'er the island dashed.

It seems as if each element
Of vengeance were the complement,
Charged with some direful punishment.

The dying wrecker raved and swore
Horrid blasphemies, 'mid the roar
And crash of tempest, on the shore.

Peering into the blackened night,
He started back in palsied fright,
As maddened by some monstrous sight—

His eyes blood-fevered, wildly turned,
As memory's fiery record burned,
Into his soul the grace long spurned.

Writhing as if a demon's stare
Fastened on him its scorching glare.
He crouched and wailed in wild despair.

And then the Phantom Ship once more,
Down on the island, blazing, bore,
And boldly swept towards the shore.

But when the wrecker breathed his last,
The tempest madly shrieked *Avast* !
And all the storm was hushed and past.

And never since that woeful night
When took that guilty soul its flight,
Has come the Phantom Ship to sight.

Setting false lights on the main land opposite Block Island, and the wreck thus caused there, ought to have had a fire-ship to punish the guilty deacon whom the poet thus describes:

THE CHARLESTOWN WRECK.

By Charles H. Denison of San Francisco.

"Below some rocks on Charlestown beach,
Almost as far as eye can reach,
Within the sweep of rolling surf,
And distant far from emerald turf,
Embedded deep in shifting sand
That fringes all the Township's land,
Are remnants of a noble ship,
Around whose ribs the algae drip,
In graceful streamers, each ebb tide,
Like Erin's banners flaunting wide;
While gurgling through her timbers stout,
The briny sea goes in and out,
Hissing and spouting all day long
In low, sad tones, a shipwreck song.

"Beyond the reach of swelling tide,
And just below the green hillside,
In years gone by an old house stood,
Its beams were made of white oak wood,
Where hard wood pins with sharpened point,
To hold more firmly mortised joint,
Were driven through the tenon's side
To keep such joints from opening wide;
While at its end outside, alone
A chimney stood, of gray-wacke stone,
To keep the mansion house upright
Through heavy tempests day and night.
Fixed in its top a stone of slate
Informed you of the builder's date.
The outside oven a child in 'teens
Might know was used for baking beans.

"The heavy outer oaken door
Directly opened on the floor;

No vestibule or 'entry' there
Protected from the gusty air,
Yet summer's sun or winter's rain,
Against its panels beat in vain.
Within its cheerful owner sat;
Beneath his chair the purring cat;
In front, and glowing at his feet,
Was piled on high the burning peat,
Diffusing warmth about the room
And dissipating winter's gloom.
Each chimney corner held a boy,
His father's pride, his mother's joy;
And cuddling there, with flaxen curl
And azure eye, a laughing girl,
Reflection of the mother fair
Who sat in her creaking old arm-chair.

"All through that day the murky skies
Had taught a lesson to the wise,
And every dweller on that shore
Had listened to the surge's roar;
Had seen with dread each hissing wave
High up the tiny sand-hills lave;
Observed the breakers foam
Far seaward with their snowy comb,
And dashing on with thundering shocks,
Break into spray on 'Noyes' Rocks.'

"In leaden sky went down the sun,
Just as the tempest had begun,
And now came fiercely o'er the main,
In dreadful gusts, the blinding rain.

"Through darkness deep, lit up by spray,
That faintly showed the dangerous way,
Reeling before the dreadful gale,
Without the vestige of a sail,
A noble ship came driving fast,
Her voyage finished, at last.

"As avalanche from mountain height,
When moving with majestic might,
Takes up the crag amid the snow,
And hurls it thundering deep below—

So this doomed ship on crested wave
Was hurled resistless to her grave,
Striking the outer bar of sand
A half mile distant from the land,
O'er which the breaking waves ran high
And threw their billows to the sky.

"Describe the scenes that there occurred,
Repeat the prayers their Maker heard,
I cannot; it would make you pale
Ere I recited half the tale:
Imagine it, all ye who can,
'Twas never told by living man.
If any heard that dreadful crash
They reckoned it the breakers' dash;
If any heard that dying wail,
They thought it shrieking of the gale—
No intermission of the roar
Of dashing rollers on the shore .
Gave evidence beneath the waves
A score of men had found their graves.
About the middle of the night
The tempest reached its utmost height,
But never failed that light to gleam,
Or from that friendly window stream,
Until the wind had died away
At ushering the 'break o' day,'

When Deacon Wilcox sought his bed
And laid to rest his nodding head.

" Like all the dwellers on the shore,
The Deacon did a wreck deplore,
With tenderness his heart o'erflowed
Toward those who on the billows rode;
His house was e'er at their command,
To them he had an open hand,
His candle on tempestuous night
Became to them a beacon-light,
A refuge also, well they knew
Was offered there to shipwrecked crew—
But inconsistency again
In Deacon's character was plain:

'Whatever comes from out the sea,'
He always said, 'belongs to me;'—
A godsend was a stranded cargo,
On which his conscience laid embargo;—

"His golden rule was *thus* applied
To waifs upon the swelling tide:—
'The ownership by him is lost
Whose goods in ship are tempest-tossed,
The ownership in him remains
Who rescues them, and who regains.'

"The Deacon slept while I've told this
In form of a parenthesis,
And ere he wakes return with me
To his old mansion by the sea.
The dreadful night at length had passed,
And cheerful daylight came at last—
Ah! never will the night be o'er
To those who floated on the shore.
The gale had sensibly decreased,
The shrieking of the wind had ceased,
But still the scuds drove through the sky,
The thundering surges yet dashed high,
Though now to all 'twas evident
The storm its force had nearly spent.

"What treasure-trove the Deacon gained
That day before the sun had waned,
I never knew, I cannot tell,
He kept his business close and well.
But afterward his oak sideboard
Had silver plate within it stored,
And oft in his spacious pocket
A watch appeared, with golden locket;
When asked if these were heirlooms old,
This story Deacon Wilcox told,
And when it was no longer new
He might have thought it almost true,—

"'As I one day walked on the beach,
The line of waves just out of reach,
I heard a strange and curious noise.
At first I thought it was my boys

Who imitate the call of birds,
The grunting swine, the lowing herds,
But looking closer at the matter
I saw it was a silver platter,
Which every time the waves did wash
Gave out the sound "slop swash! slop swash!"

" 'Another day I walked along
The sandy beach and hummed a song,
Heard something go 'tick, whiz! tick, whiz!'
Looked down and saw a watch-like phiz;
I snatched it from the moistened sand,
And when I had it in my hand
I saw a time-piece, quaint and old,
Its face and cases, British gold,
And well it was I came that way,
It had been spoiled another day.'

" These stories of the watch and platter
Were always sure to end the matter—
The questioner polite receded—
He had the information needed."

In the foregoing extract from Mr. Denison's poem entitled "*Rhode Island*," we find it strongly insinuated that on the main shore of Block Island Sound, as well as "over the rocky Head," false lights were set for wrecking vessels. Supposing this to be true, may we not also suppose it to have been a cunning shift in the Charlestown people, to say of the Islanders, as Mr. Congdon did,—"Nobody doubted her [the fire-ship] being sent by an Almighty Power to punish those wicked men"? Was she not sent to punish the "wicked men" of Charlestown who saw her so frequently, and had such deep convictions of her awful mission? Perhaps some wicked man over there died a few minutes before the Palatine Light went out for the last time.

SCHOOLS OF BLOCK ISLAND.

The first one of which we have any account was located a little east of the north end of Fresh Pond, and was a common school in which were taught the alphabet, spelling, reading, writing, and arithmetic. It existed when it was a frequent occurrence for men to sign a paper by each making his "mark."

The next school was opened on the Neck, and according to tradition was quite largely attended, and was conducted in the usual manner of schools on the main land. These have been followed by others, one on the West Side, one near the Harbor, and one at the Gulley. All the old houses of these five schools have disappeared, and new ones with modern improvements have been substituted. But few populations of less than twelve hundred have sustained five schools in a better condition. In 1857 in the School Commissioner's Report it was said of them: —"They are as good schools as those in any of the country towns in the State."

The Island High School, at the Center, was opened for the first time Nov. 29, 1875, by Mr. Arthur W. Brown, of Middletown, R. I., with sixteen pupils during the first term. After several terms of successful studies under its first principal, as he left the Island, highly esteemed by many warm friends, the school has continued to prosper under the management of its present principal, Mr. C. E. Perry, a native of the Island. As an act of encouragement the town gave to the school the free use of the Town Hall. One of its graduates, Mr. Clarence Littlefield, is now a student in Brown University, and others have become teachers, and are preparing for college.

THE ISLAND LIBRARY.

The first action for its establishment was on March 6, 1875, by the inauguration of "The Island Library Association," at the office of Dr. T. H. Mann, who was chosen president. By the efforts of friends of the enterprise, especially of Mr. A. W. Brown, its librarian, contributions of money and books were obtained within two years to make the number of volumes on its shelves in the Town Hall more than five hundred. Donations of books from visitors of means and friends of learning would be well appropriated on this Island, by increasing its library.

PRESIDENT GRANT'S VISIT.

While many men of eminence have visited Block Island, no one has done it more honor by a brief stay there than did President Grant, on the 18th of August, 1875. In compliance with an invitation from Hon. Nicholas Ball, of the Island, extended to him through Senators H.B. Anthony and Maj.-Gen. Burnside, the President, accompanied by his Secretary Bristow, Attorney-General Pierrepont, and Senators Anthony and Burnside, spent a few hours on the Island, dining at the Ocean View Hotel, where he shook hands with a respectable number, and after riding about some time went aboard the revenue cutter *Grant*, which steamed and sailed off at 3 P. M. with her tall and graceful three masts for Cape May.

ISLAND CHURCHES.

No church was immediately organized at the time the Island was settled by its little colony of sixteen families from Massachusetts. But they carried with them the fundamental principles of a Christian society. Before they set foot upon the Island they united in setting apart a considerable portion of it to be forever known and used as the "Ministers Land," and for more than two centuries it has been devoted to the support of the Christian religion. They were kindred to Roger Williams, spiritually, and afterward by marriage, and he frequently associated with its early settlers. During a period of ninety years the venerable Simon Ray, and his son Simon, Jr., as lay preachers, without ordination, without salary, or meeting-house, conducted public worship among their townsmen, during a part of which time the same was done by the influential Capt. James Sands. His grandson, Samuel Niles, in his accounts of the first settlers of the Island, where he was born, has incidently given the religious characteristics of those settlers. He, as the first student from Rhode Island to enter college, after graduating at Harvard, returned to the Island a Congregationalist, and there, a licentiate, officiated as the first settled minister. Mr. Niles, fifty years pastor at Braintree, Mass., said of his grandfather Sands:—"He was the leading man among them." "He also was a promoter of religion in his benefactions to the minister they had there in his day, though not altogether so agreeable to him as he might be desired, as *being inclined to the Anabaptist persuasion.*" By this is meant that Mr. Sands was a Baptist, and disagreed with his Congregationalist preacher, his own grandson. "He devoted his house for the worship of God, where it was attended every Lord's day or Sabbath," and the Hon. Wm. P. Sheffield of Newport, a native of the Island, says of Mr. Sands that "he did not differ in religious belief from the other settlers." As their "belief" at that time was very uncongenial to the prevailing "belief" in Massachusetts whence they emigrated, and where there was an abundance of land for them, we find the probable reason for their going to a remote Island then inhabited only by savages. *There* they were safer than in the colony from which they saw others banished. *There* they could enjoy more in the possession of "soul liberty" than they could at Braintree and Boston where men and women were persecuted for their religion.

The first call to a minister, on the Island, was made in

March, 1700, not by a church but by the town, at a regular meeting, where a preamble equivalent to a brief sermon was signed by twenty-eight freemen, ten by "his mark." This preamble deeded to him "five acres, giving the right and disposition thereof to Samuel Niles and his heirs forever." He accepted the call, accepted the land, but either he as a disciple of Harvard College was not acceptable to his Baptist hearers, or they were not congenial to him, and he sold his land and settled in Braintree, where he was ordained May 23, 1711.

A missionary period of about fifty years, with perhaps short pastorates, seems to have intervened between the resignation of Mr. Niles and another permanent settlement of a minister. In 1756 Rev. Samuel Maxwell, a Baptist ordained in Swansea, Mass., Apr. 18, 1733, received part of the rents of the "Ministry Lot," and in Sept., 1758, he received from the Island £124, "old tenor," "for his serving as a minister in said town the last four months." This was by vote at a town meeting. The "Ministry Lot," in 1756, rented for "£400, old tenor," and this sum was equivalent to $50.00, and Mr. Maxwell's appropriation from the town in 1758 was $15.50.

The Island religion was indicated in a town vote Aug. 28, 1759, to employ Rev. David Sprague "so long as said Sprague shall serve the inhabitants of the town by preaching to them the gospel of Christ according to the Scriptures of truth, making them, and them only the rules of his faith, doctrine, and practice." He complied with these terms fifteen years, until he moved from the Island in the summer of 1775.

The first church on the Island was organized under Mr. Sprague's ministry. He had been ordained on the 12th of July, 1739. At an adjourned meeting, Oct. 3, 1772, the organization was affected. They had previously drawn up articles of faith and practice. Their services, though brief, were comprehensive and solemn. The minister, four brethren, and three sisters were assembled, and "then read the articles of fellowship with one another, and then the church gave Elder Sprague the right hand of fellowship to administer the ordinances of God as an evangelist." Three months afterward, for the appointment of a deacon, the pastor, at a meeting, called upon each brother " to pass single before the Lord to see whether there was one in the church that was called of God to the office of a deacon." Thomas Dodge, in doing so, expressed the conviction of his call to that service. Then the pastor "met him in a covenant way and declared that he believed that his dedication was of God, and gave him fellowship in the office of deacon." While holding this office during the Revolution, without a pastor, until 1784, he gained "a good degree," for he was then ordained as the successor of Mr. Sprague.

For a view of the succession of pastors of this church, articles of faith, etc., see History of Block Island.

A Free-Will Baptist Church was organized on the Island about the year 1820, and also a *Seventh-Day Baptist Church*, in April, 1864, although it has had no house of worship.

One of the remarkable things of Block Island is that while the Christian religion has been well represented here more than two hundred years, in an average population of over 1,000 during the last hundred years, only one denomination has here existed, while the members of the first church at one time were over four hundred, and those of the other two were one hundred and fifty. On this Island neither sprinkling, nor pouring, nor signing of the cross for baptism; nor human grades of ecclesiastical authority have ever been recognized by its inhabitants.

The Meeting-Houses of the Island have indicated a commendable zeal for religion. After having held their meetings at the private houses of Simon Ray and his son, and of Capt. James Sands about ninety years, they built their *first* house of worship near the north end, and easterly of the Fresh Pond, of which the Rev. Dr. Stiles said, in 1756, the houses of the Island were, "all but two or three, within two and a half miles of the meeting-house." From this the sparseness of the population on the Neck then may be inferred.

The second meeting-house of the first church was built in 1814, and was located on Cemetery Hill, "similar and equal in appearance to those of others of the country towns of the state." It had "the old square pews and sounding board," and was erected by the town, as was its predecessor. It was subsequently moved, rebuilt, and has since been occupied as the Town Hall, and latterly also as the High School building.

The third meeting-house of said church was located on Gravel Hill, incorrectly called *Graves* Hill in the History of the Island. It stood a little east of the Center, on the north side of the road from the Harbor to the Center, and on the first little hill east of the Center. It was built "on shares," and was occupied until the year 1857.

The fourth meeting-house of the first church was dedicated on the 25th of August, 1863, at which time the steamer Canonicus conveyed from Providence and Newport eleven hundred passengers, then " one of the largest and most agreeable steamboat excursions ever known." This house cost $2,500, most of the funds having been procured by the energy of the pastor, *Rev. Albert Gladwin.* The first furnace ever seen upon the Island was placed in this house in 1875. The sailor phrases applied to this novelty, if recorded, would afford much amusement.

The first Free-Will meeting-house, on the West Side, was erected in the year 1853, and was burned in the year 1863. The *second* one was partially built in 1869, but was demolished by the great September gale of that year. It was intended to be like the one now at the Center. The *third* house erected by the Free-Will Baptists is the one which they now occupy.

Seven houses of worship, as seen from the foregoing, have been erected on Block Island since it was settled. What population that has never equaled fifteen hundred has done better? Too many have judged of the Islanders as unfairly as they would to characterize the entire city of Boston by the habits of a few of its worst sailors and fanatics.

Rev. W. A. Durfee is the present pastor of the First Baptist church of the Island, at the Center, and *Rev. Geo. Wheeler* is pastor of the Free Will Baptist Church on the West Side.

Breinigsville, PA USA
10 October 2010
247047BV00005B/102/P